SIXTEEN MILLION ONE

Understanding Civil War

◆ ◆ ◆

Patrick M. Regan

Paradigm Publishers
Boulder ◆ London

Copyright © 2009 Paradigm Publishers

Published in the United States by Paradigm Publishers, 3360 Mitchell Lane Suite E, Boulder, CO 80301 USA.

Paradigm Publishers is the trade name of Birkenkamp & Company, LLC, Dean Birkenkamp, President and Publisher.

Library of Congress Cataloging-in-Publication Data

Regan, Patrick M.
  Sixteen million one : understanding civil war / Patrick M. Regan.
    p. cm. — (International studies intensives)
  Includes bibliographical references.
  ISBN 978-1-59451-619-1 (hardcover : alk. paper)
  1. Insurgency. 2. Civil war. I. Title.
  JC328.5.R44 2009
  303.6′4—dc22
                                                                    2008027599

Printed and bound in the United States of America on acid-free paper that meets the standards of the American National Standard for Permanence of Paper for Printed Library Materials.

Designed and typeset by Straight Creek Bookmakers.

13 12 11 10 09   1 2 3 4 5

To Umi and Kaitlin

CONTENTS

ACKNOWLEDGMENTS

Many thanks are in order. Binghamton University provided sabbatical time for me to write most of this book; the Fulbright Foundation provided funding for an extended stay in Norway. The Peace Research Institute of Oslo (PRIO) and the Center for the Study of Civil Wars, in particular Scott Gates and Nils Petter Gleditsch, provided a great environment for my stay. The National Science Foundation and the World Bank each provided funding for some of the research that shapes the arguments I present. I thank Bobbie Lord, Celeste Rabaut, Wendy Martinek, Fritz Johnson, and Meg Mitzel, my spouse, for providing commentary along the way, and in Meg's case for a good dose of tolerance. Shane and Kaitlin Regan, my children, deserve thanks for imploring me to wear a bulletproof vest on my trip to Palestine, and for not fully accepting my answer that it was neither necessary nor practical. It was one of the ways they showed me that they care. I owe a note of thanks to Will Moore for introducing me to Umi Deshpande, and I owe a huge debt of gratitude to Umi for answering a rather arcane email from a stranger, one that she could have just as easily put in the "trash." In the end Umi stuck with me and provided more than most would think wise, read more drafts than anybody would think sane, and taught me more about writing with emotion than I ever thought would be useful. I dedicate this effort to Umi for all she contributed, and to Kaitlin who blurted out one night at the dinner table, "What am I supposed to tell my friends? That my dad is going off to be killed by terrorists?" Honey, they're not terrorists, just people with few options who try to make change by force of arms. Unfortunately there are many people in similar predicaments. Maybe someday you can be part of the process that changes the way the world works.

Patrick M. Regan

1

♦ ♦ ♦

SIXTEEN MILLION

is the number of people who have died in civil wars in the last fifty years. Give or take a person.

Every generation has its civil war. Mine was Cambodia, 1978. This war accounts for at least a million of those sixteen by some estimates. The famine that ensued in the war's aftermath took its own toll, starving the displaced millions that had survived the killing fields of the Angkar. The American Red Cross, the UN, the world community began to respond to the humanitarian crisis that was developing. I was in my first year of college, studying to be an airline pilot. But Cambodia happened, and I wanted to be there. I wanted to help in some way. The relief agencies needed truck drivers, and I had just quit driving a truck to go to college. I hitchhiked to Detroit to meet my father, to tell him my intentions. We sat in a diner drinking endless refills of the same cup of coffee, and I attempted to convince him that it was imperative I go to Cambodia. He listened, as fathers do. But he cautioned me to "stay in college. There will be other wars for you, and other famines." He was right, as fathers are. Although I could hardly stomach the idea then, of other wars and other famines, of millions starving and dead, there have been, of course, other wars and other famines. Many other wars and many other famines. What my father said came not from callousness, as I had then imagined, but from knowing what I now know. That civil wars happen, that famines follow them, that we have not learned how to stop, or manage, let alone prevent civil wars. And so, every generation has its civil war. Or two or three. The Rwandan and Sudanese wars have killed about a million people each, Uganda a quarter of a million, Bosnia two hundred thousand, Indonesia three hundred thousand, the Philippines between fifty and sixty thousand. Cambodia, Yugoslavia, and today, Iraq. And there are those that go on unrelenting, sometimes silent, sometimes boiling, simmering through generation after generation—Northern Ireland, Sri Lanka, Kashmir, Palestine.

In hindsight, and with a decade of research behind me, it is clear to me that civil wars are neither isolated nor unique events. There have been, in the last fifty years, on average twenty civil wars ongoing in each year. The lands, the people, the very spirit of the countries they are fought in are left ruined, exhausted, unable to resurrect themselves for generations, and some have slipped back into war again and again. In 1978 I did not want to face the reality that these events would outlast me, and I have been puzzled ever since about why wars happen and what we can do to prevent them. They seem like such an outmoded means of settling disagreements, and yet even the wisest, the wealthiest, and the most informed appear to walk willingly into the carnage in pursuit of some outcome that could be achieved without sacrificing the lives of so many people. Over the years I've found that there are no easy answers, nor are there easy solutions. I have become convinced, however, that wars are neither necessary nor inevitable. Civil wars may be the most perplexing of all wars to comprehend, and yet, they are most influenced by attempts to control them. Commonplace and as devastating as they are, though, civil wars are little understood by the public, by the media, even by the very policy makers who make a difference in the outcomes of these wars. Just look at the debate about whether Iraq is or is not in a civil war. Thousands of people die each month because organized and armed groups are fighting over control, and we cannot come to grips with whether or not we should *call* this a civil war. If the implications were not so important we wouldn't be discussing the issue on the cable news, nor would it have been an election issue.

It is only by understanding the causes of civil wars that policy makers can design effective ways to control them. We can talk about anticipating genocides, eliminating dictators, preventive interventions, and eradicating poverty, but unless there is a clear grasp of how and why these issues arise, coherent policies cannot be developed. It is the broad public—you and I—who has to bear the burden of the outcomes, and we need, therefore, to have clear ideas about the causes and the implications.

The two weeks before Christmas 2006, I spent in the Palestinian Territories, behind the Israeli separation wall. A wall is a special kind of structure. It has the purpose of keeping someone, or something, in or out. I state the obvious, but it occurred to me in that way, as I stood before this behemoth, in shock and awe at the sheer, gray, forbidding size of it. It reminded me of nothing so much as the barricades surrounding any gated community, between any elite compound and overflowing ghetto. This wall, this security fence, is nothing more than a big brother, a large-scale replica, of those glass-studded walls that separate villas from shantytowns, bungalows from slums, anywhere and everywhere in the world. The Israelis have their justification, but to see it is something else. It divides, as those other walls do, the elite, the politically powerful, from those without access. Walls mean confinement. Those on the other side are certainly confined. The wall itself is a symbol to the Palestinians, a sign of their frustration, and in many ways it seems to them to legitimize their call of injustice, and their call to arms.

I was in Palestine to try to meet with those who have chosen to take up arms against the Israeli occupation, armed resistance fighters who risk everything in pursuit of political change. The war between Hezbollah and Israel had just ended. The fighting in Gaza had intensified. U.S. fatalities in Iraq had crossed the three thousand mark. I wanted to reconfirm my intuitions. I wanted to put all my scholarly evidence and arguments on the cold ground of reality. My intention was to renew my understanding of that individual who confronts, each day, the inequities of poverty and hunger, of social and political discrimination, the individual who lives every day with very little hope of redress. I was there because I felt that a book about civil wars would not be complete without the voice of those who have chosen armed resistance, those who have chosen a route with little hope of immediate success and a very high chance of their being killed in the process.

We hear it said again and again that there is no justification for violence. That those who choose that path are inherently evil, full of hatred and murder. I wasn't looking for justification. I have over a decade of study into civil wars and the experience and intuition of life, and of being in situations of conflict. I do know that this choice to take up arms is virtually the same for the villager in Darfur being pushed from his land, or the Palestinian walled into a prison, as it would be for you or me.

I have asked myself this question many times over the years: under what conditions would I leave my family, my job, all of my life as I know it, to take on the life of a rebel soldier? That, after all, is what it comes down to. A man or woman—a single individual—must make that decision, and then take several dangerous steps before he has become a rebel soldier. People just like you and me fight in civil wars. A man who runs a grocery store with his brother, teenagers who loiter at street corners trading insults and cigarettes, a young woman struggling with med school. Ordinary people. Civilians, not trained soldiers. People, like you and me. What drives people to make that decision? What would bring me to that point? What would bring you to that point? I wanted to be able to get into the head of that individual, and to be able to think about his situation, his future, through his eyes. I needed to understand the gravity of the risk that rebels take. I wanted to feel the fear that must come with the choice to take up arms against my government. The risks that I was taking in order to gain this perspective seemed worth it.

I could have chosen from among a lot of different war zones to meet with armed rebels, to witness to some small extent the conditions that drive them to that point. I chose Palestine for two basic reasons: I know that some conflicts are more central to Western conscious-ness than others, and I am convinced that the root of each conflict is basically the same, or at least has a similar set of processes. This, then, is a well-known conflict, and one where the conditions in the Occupied Territories mirror those in other civil wars. To some this is not a civil war but an anticolonial struggle, but I looked past the finer details of whether or not liberation struggles are civil wars and whether or not Israel and the Palestinian Territories are two separate states or one, in large part because of the centrality of my personal security.

Safety, my own safety, that is, was my second major criterion. In Palestine I thought I could get in, find my way to the armed rebels, and get out alive. I knew about the recent spate of kidnappings, but up to this point not one kidnapped Westerner had been killed. I was also aware of the risk from an Israeli incursion or missile strike if I happened to be in the vicinity of those they want to assassinate. Which, of course, was exactly where I wanted to be.

This is not the first time I have been in a war zone or taken such personal risks. But this time, what I had to risk was substantial. I have two children and a wife, all of whom I wanted to see again. The last thing I wanted to do was push the idea of risk too far. But my level of risk didn't even approach that of those I met who were part of the armed resistance. One Palestinian told me that there was, literally, no going home once on that road, because the Israelis would assassinate you. At the extreme of this road to rebellion are the suicide bombers of Iraq, Sri Lanka, and Palestine.

The men I met in Palestine were just some of the thousands around the world who choose to take up arms to fight their country-men. They could have been Sri Lankan, Sudanese, Burmese, Indian, Congolese, or Kurdish. They all make this same choice; they are all confronted with similar circumstances of poverty, disparity, or political impotence. They all leave their homes, families, and the life they know to go down another, dangerous path with few ways back. But it is a path that they choose in spite of knowing the risks. We can't really understand civil wars unless we can understand why they take this risk.

In Palestine, every adult I met worried that their son would be recruited to the armed resistance, and every adult knew someone whose child was. But in spite of the fact that everyone worried, everyone also thought that this horrible prospect was a distinct possibility, because of the brutality of the occupation. One afternoon I sat in the house of a man who had spent over twenty years in Israeli prisons, accused of being a cell leader for the Islamic Jihad. Although he wouldn't directly "confess" to me, he lucidly described the tactics, training, and rules that went with participation. When I asked if his sixteen-year-old son—his only child—should join the resistance, he simply shrugged. Fighting the occupation was apparently more important than the life of his son. The taxi driver who took me to Ramallah shrugged the same way when I asked about his thirteen-year-old son. The feeling was ubiquitous.

To a man, those I asked said that they had nothing against the Israeli individual, but the government that was the occupier had to go. There was no middle ground on that score. Whether these people who take up arms are from Palestine, or Burma, or Sri Lanka, the basic underlying causes for their struggle are the same: poverty and inequities born of discrimination of the political, social, or religious variants. There is the humiliation of standing at checkpoints, the grief and rage of having your children killed for throwing stones, being shot for resisting the encroachment onto traditional lands. There is political impoverishment that leads directly to economic impoverishment.

Poverty presents for us a moral dilemma. Wealth amongst the impoverished makes the wealthy look—and quite often feel—bad. Guilty. Policies of redistribution are just political choices, but since the wealthy tend to hold the reins of political power, they choose not to address questions of poverty in ways that infringe on their wealth. There are several rationales for this, most based on the notion that if the few create vast wealth, eventually some of it will trickle down to help those less fortunate. It never seems to work that way, but some stand behind this theory. The impoverished will eventually act, either by developing the political access that facilitates the redistribution or by dint of the gun.

Many people recognize the moral dilemma of poverty. Bono and Oprah champion the eradication of poverty because of its moral boundaries. Poverty amid wealth is the problem, one we can all recognize and react to, at least in the abstract. But when these boundaries encroach upon our own private goods, the risks increase dramatically and we tend to retract completely. The moral repulsion to poverty confronts us with the question of how much we will be willing to give up in order to abide by our moral compulsion. This takes poverty from being a moral dilemma into being a very practical one. Because when those who feel structurally deprived reach the point of being willing to risk all that they have—even if what they have is quite meager—for the prospects of change, they make the elite face the ethical question of whether they will give up some of what they have or fight to keep it. In effect fight for continued poverty. Imagine the arguments we have to come up with to justify fighting to maintain poverty! Now that is a real moral dilemma. And one that is all around us.

We have confronted the scourge of poverty on many dimensions for many years. Much of our collective effort does not really address the core causes of poverty—the politics and the discrimination—but we do an amazingly good job of sending money, giving aid, opening food pantries, televising the human tragedy, and hoping that it will all go away, or at least stay away from us. Often when we give aid to relieve poverty it is the wealthy in the impoverished countries who steal it. To put it bluntly, sometimes the West indirectly helps to enrich the elite in these impoverished countries, who in turn repress their citizens when they demand more—more access, more opportunity, more of what others have. President Mobutu of Zaire is the classic example of aid going to a despot in a desperately poor country. The giving of aid, the stocking of food pantries, the "adopting a child" generally reflect responses based on the moral dilemma with which poverty confronts us.

But in truth, poverty presents an entirely different kind of dilemma, one that is much more practical than moral. The dilemma is the risk to stability that results from civil wars, civil wars that result from structural poverty. I use as an example the young Palestinian men walled into the West Bank and willing to admit to a stranger that they are part of the armed struggle. Theirs is an example of choices made by young men who simply lost options that were nonviolent.

Their choice now is the pursuit of change down the barrel of a gun, and they risk everything for that dim hope of change. They don't have a lot to risk, but it is all on the line.

Choosing to join a rebellion must be considered relative to other options that are available to each disgruntled individual. Each of the young men I met could have chosen to nonviolently protest the occupation, the separation wall, the confiscation of land. They chose instead to side with those using force to challenge Israeli policy. I met many others who had made different choices. In fact the nonviolent opposition to Israeli policy is remarkably strong given the conditions under which it operates. And the nonviolent opponents get considerable support from internationalists and Israelis who do not support the occupation. These two groups of people made vastly different choices. If all those who confronted an oppressive government deliberately chose the path of nonviolence to challenge authority, there would be no civil wars. Political movements, yes, but not civil wars.

The fact that we have so many civil wars around the world means that many people are choosing to take up arms, to embrace the most risky strategy possible, one with very low odds of success and very high costs for participation. By my reading of the situation in the Palestinian Territories the two groups divide largely along different social and economic conditions. In Palestine I found that those who have some wealth—in spite of the occupation and abuse—generally take a nonviolent approach to resistance. Those who are more materially deprived, those who occupy the refugee camps, those without jobs, those who spend time in Israeli prisons, take the violent approach. They have little left to lose. Sometimes the humiliation and loss are so extreme that even those who are not materially deprived will choose a path of violent opposition. A young woman, a lawyer, in Haifa, Israel, is but one example. Israeli raids killed her brother, her fiancé, and her uncle, and she lost all hope or reason to live. She strapped herself with explosives and blew herself up in a café.

Poor people will resist. Not all of them, not all today, but their time will come. People can be impoverished in a number of ways, but most lead right back to the ability to eke out a living that is acceptable, up to some standard that is consistent with the society in which they live. People or groups can be politically impoverished, shut out of any political influence that might allow them to get ahead on any number of economic and social dimensions. Being shut out of opportunities to act as a community can also culturally impoverish people. And yes, people can just be downright poor, unable to provide for themselves or their family, with life always existing at the margins. Any small bump in their fortunes can turn a poor existence into a struggle for survival. This type of poverty that we all generally think of—the financial struggle to survive—is quite often linked to the other types of poverty—those of the political, social, or cultural variety. People who are shut out of political processes also tend to be excluded from economic opportunities; those cultural groups who suffer discrimination on the basis of language or race tend also to be discriminated against when they pursue economic opportunities. There is, eventually, recognition of this kind of structure that keeps groups of people poor. And at some point, people will try, somehow, to change that structure. In the most extreme cases they take up arms against those who impose these conditions upon them, to bring down those walls.

There are compelling reasons to prevent future wars, and to manage and stop ongoing wars or the ones that were not possible to prevent. A civil war is a war in which those fighting are from the same country. But this describes only the end result of a long process. The conditions that lead people to take up arms against their government, to engage in violent attacks against their military, to risk their lives for change, must be such that the risky alternative of armed conflict becomes acceptable. Civil wars begin quietly, in the daily lives of people. Poverty and inequities pile hardship upon hunger on people living at the margins. It wears them down day after day, pushing them to the wall, to despair, to anger, to insurrection. The unspeakable spasm of violence that gripped Rwanda, for example, a slaughter that summons images of machetes and bodies flowing downriver for two whole months, was not the start of civil war. Civil wars are often the final acts of decades of the slow agony of political and social discrimination, of hunger, of endless poverty, of little hope, so little that the risk of death while fighting seems better than slow death under unacceptable conditions.

Solutions are often hard to come by, particularly when the root causes are tied to such fundamental processes—the creation of wealth and power relationships. But short-term steps can be taken to cut short those wars that have started and impede the steps to war in those countries at risk. The United States and others intervene in ongoing civil wars, sometimes to the benefit, and sometimes to the detriment, of those involved. The United States in particular has the clout, monetary and political, to negotiate settlements, offer incentives, change the course of the future. The reason for me to write this book is, of course, to explain the workings of civil wars, but also to dispel some of the myths associated with them. I hope that this will give people a better idea of what they allow or encourage their government to do, or what it implies when they back a foreign policy in the name of bringing freedom to some country that may not understand it in our terms. Or to at least be able to question, coherently, what cause their sons and daughters are being sent overseas to fight for, perhaps never to return.

As an academic, I can speak of the mechanics of war. But in doing so, I hope to provoke thought about what civil war is and what it does to us as a community. Not just to the people who are at war, but to those of us who are not. Reducing the amount of violence within countries will be akin to the environmental issues that former vice president Al Gore champions. To his mind environmental sensitivity is the issue of our time and the response will take a lot of individuals to be more involved, to reduce their energy footprint. In effect, to address the problems of global warming by each individual taking small steps. Those small steps start with learning about the problem and end with taking action to try to alleviate the consequences of our environmental abuse. I want to put on that table the idea that internal instability in countries around the world is yet another of those issues of our time, that we cannot talk in terms of a global society while thousands are taking up arms to fight for a better opportunity.

It may well be that we can only take small steps and make small changes, but history tells us that nothing is fated or unchangeable. Things are not today as they were yesterday, and can be changed in the smallest ways so that they will be different tomorrow. To not make the small changes because we do not have the silver bullets, to refuse to tackle a problem because it looks too big, is only to let it get bigger. We are just learning the enormous implications of this benign neglect as the glaciers melt and our oceans rise.

In an era of global markets, world travel, instantaneous television reporting, and worldwide migration, we have an abiding interest in global stability. It harms all of us to have some of us living under conditions in which armed rebellion is the best opportunity available. It does no good to talk of global societies, free trade zones, world production platforms, and exotic vacations if political instability is shifting the range of possible locations for trade, production, or tourism. The moral dilemma of poverty in the midst of wealth will confront our ideals about the opening of the world to trade and ideas. If the poor of the world continue to rise up against the inequitable distribution of wealth, then the rest of us will have to confront the choice of supporting the oppression, supporting the rebels, or doing nothing. None of these are good options and each tarnishes our conceptions of civil society and an enlightened society in a global village.

CAUSES

2

♦ ♦ ♦

DISCONTENT

Quilali, Nicaragua, 1986, was in the midst of a civil war. The town had the aura of fear, of the uncertainty of life in the time of war, of the hopelessness and resignation in the face of the void that had replaced their future. Young men were absent from the streets. The only ones I saw were the soldiers in my hotel, young men with old faces and new weapons. Sandinista soldiers. I spent the evening in that edge-of-town motel, handling their AK-47s, trading things, talking about the government army's rules of engagement with the insurgents. Sometime that night the unmistakable crackling of automatic weapons fire startled me out of a fitful sleep. Gunfire erupted in the jungles at the perimeter of the town, and I crouched down on the dirt floor of my room hoping that no errant bullets would come my way, hoping that the walls were strong enough to keep them out. There I was, all warnings unheeded, drowning in the thrill of being in a war zone. I had discovered where all the young men of the town had gone. The next morning the soldiers, too, were gone. The road out of Quilali was notorious for rebel ambushes, so I left with trepidation, but a sense of puzzlement most of all. What did it take? What made a man leave the world he knew in pursuit of change when that pursuit might cost him his life?

Discontent. The realization that things are not fated to be any one way. That life can be changed. The intolerable conditions of daily life. The desire for a better future, or at least a different future. These things do not always motivate people to take action. When you live your life in hardship each day, sometimes it is something you accept as your lot. But when you confront what you lack each day, when you see that someone else does not live with that void simply because of the color of their skin or their choice of religion or some other accident of birth that separates you from them in wealth and power, then that void is harder to accept, those emotions are perhaps harder to push away.

The sequence then may be discontent, resentment, bitterness, anger. And perhaps one day there is a man, or woman, who articulates this anger in terms of action, in terms of possible change. A person who pinpoints the place, the person, the system on which to lay the blame. Someone who takes on the discontent of hundreds and conveys it as righteous anger, and then demands justice. And all of the resentment, anger, envy, and desire run together and acquire a meaning. And individuals, like drops of rain, become a flood. The flood, the outrage, channeled by the dams and levees of leadership, now has direction and deadly purpose. An individual with the weapon of resentment and the ammunition of anger, when brought together with other such individuals, rebel soldiers in a rebel army, will take their country to civil war in the pursuit of change. Not always, and not always in the same way. But it happens, more often than it should.

This process moves the anger into rebellion and it runs through efforts to protest conditions, to demand changes, to implement reforms, to make conditions better without having to first make them worse through an armed struggle. But protest ignored or repressed does worse than the simple pangs of poverty alone.

Poverty of the sort that leads to rebellion is an enigma wrapped in a dilemma with consequences that at times seem disproportional to the problem at hand. This is the moral dilemma we face. Poverty, by many accounts, has always existed. There have always been people poorer than other people in the same community, and that remains so. But it is the poverty born of intention, the poverty that results from policies designed to create wealth, not for all but for a select group, that drives the engine of frustration. And if these policies create wealth for some and frustration for others, then fighting to maintain those policies and this structure can be seen as socially bankrupt. An example of the idea of poverty by design is the history of black people in the United States. Blacks were made poor by intent by a system set up to work against this one group of people. Initially it was through the scourge of slavery, but when that was forced to end, it was continued through institutionalized policies, policies upheld even by the Supreme Court. Blacks were poor by design because many whites condoned the system that kept them poor. The system was intentional. The legacy—and some would say the policies—still hold sway today.

In a small building in a refugee camp in the West Bank, I met, among others, Walid. He and the other resistance fighters in the room described the area to me as the largest walled prison in the world. Having gone through that wall, I understand perfectly well why they think that. To them the wall symbolizes the intentional policy that will keep them subservient, that will keep them always at the margins of subsistence relying on the goodwill of the world community to provide food and shelter. But only for as long as the Israelis permit it. The world community recognizes their plight and provides the sustenance, because it is morally repugnant to have people suffering at the margins. But the world community doesn't act on the structure, and that is what turned a group of otherwise normal young men into armed rebels fighting the Israeli occupation. This same type of structure is what gets the black Sudanese man from Darfur to take up arms against the government controlled by the Arabs and enforced by the Janjaweed militia.

The men I met were all in their twenties. Young men living a hard life. They were all born in the local refugee camp to which their grandparents had fled after the war with Israel, and where their parents were raised. All they have ever known is the squalid life of this refugee camp. This is a place the Israeli military attacks with great regularity, and when they do, Walid and his comrades fight back as best they can. If not for the largesse of the outside world these young men and their families would be destitute. But it is also in part because of the world community that they are relegated to this camp, that they are poor by any objective standard, and that they hold little hope for change as a result of a political process. Not all the people in the camp reject the idea of change through a political process, but Walid and the young men with him certainly do. And in an odd sort of a way they have evidence on their side. As these young men described it to me, they are impoverished by virtue of a system that dictates that they have no income and no hope of meaningful change on that score. They are also impoverished because they are cut out of any political decisions that determine their fate. That is, they are materially impoverished because they are politically impoverished. But they also bemoan the fact that they are socially impoverished. They know that they are viewed by the world community as dirty, dumb, and violent, and that their worth is considered to be lower than that of the European Israelis who occupy their territory. To nearly the entire world—and certainly under international law—the West Bank is Palestinian territory occupied by Israel. Contemporary media portray the Palestinian as violent and in some sense inferior to the Israeli, and in that regard less worthy of land, rights, or freedom. It is this structure, one reinforced by the powerful and imposed on the weak, that perpetuates the refugee camp system in Palestine, as it does to so many dispossessed around the world. One of the men said to me that his people would end up like the American Indians—abused, marginalized, and then forgotten. Forestalling such a fate, to them, is worth fighting for.

While all of what these armed men said to me might not be empirically correct, and I have no immediate way to corroborate it all, if these are their perceptions, or expectations, then to them the future holds little if they play by the rules. Fighting for change provides a viable alternative, albeit one fraught with incredible risk.

These issues are much more general than just the Palestinian struggle against the Israeli occupation, and in many ways describe the moral struggles we face. How does the world community in this age of vast wealth and information continue to avoid questions of structural poverty, of structural inequities? Even if we reject the notion of a moral imperative, we ought to consider whether structural poverty is simply bad for business. The grand sweep of the market may be more costly than we think. There are countless Walids in this world, and a key to reducing armed conflict is to remove the incredibly strained conditions that create the incentives for the young men like him who confront the choice of whether or not to resist their government.

So what are the situations that cause people to despise the conditions of their very existence? What is the language that describes the situation that leads an individual to choose to fight those who live in the same country? What causes an individual to give up the life they know and take up arms, to turn onto a road full of such danger and uncertainty in order to make a difference, particularly when the path they take provides conditions worse than those they reject? Poverty, the data show, is at the heart of it. Poverty, in its many forms. Some are obvious and unmistakable—the starving child, somewhere on the dark continent, the ubiquitous flies in its eyes. The sprawling slums of Rio de Janeiro. The destitute of Calcutta. Some forms of poverty are quiet, hidden in the lives of the people who live it until something happens to thrust it into the forefront of collective consciousness. The residents of New Orleans' Ninth Ward waiting days, while the whole world held its breath in disbelief, for some help from their own government. The long lines of refugees streaming out of Darfur, away from the fast-tightening grip of war. And the poverty of those for whom the only hope after years of being prisoners in their own land is in the eyes of dead martyrs looking down on them. They haunt the narrow, crowded alleyways of Gaza, San Salvador, and Addis Ababa.

And there is the not so obvious poverty. Neither the Catholics of Northern Ireland nor the people of northern Nicaragua were destitute, or even on the verge of it. Theirs was a type of poverty born of frustration with a system that discriminates. Those fighting the government were the ones who were losing on economic, social, and political dimensions, at least relative to the other groups in their communities. It is not the level or type of poverty that is most important, ultimately, but what the people feel who live those lives. How they respond to the situation they find themselves in. The man in Belfast, Derry, or Ulster may not be poor compared to the one in Calcutta. But faced with the despotism of the dominant majority, or minority, to which he did not belong, he joined his fellow aggrieved in a bid to change what he could, and take back what he considered his right. The beggar in Calcutta lives his life, though much poorer than the man in Belfast, with resignation and acceptance, perhaps because there is no place to lay the blame for it, and no one to direct that upheaval. The man in Calcutta is hungry, but so is everyone else around him.

We, as academics, as social scientists, categorize and subcategorize everything in order to better understand, in order to study. To us, there are data that show that a country has low national wealth, high infant mortality rates, poor or no healthcare, and short life expectancy. A person who lives in such a country at the margins of survival lives the reality of this poverty. She has to struggle to make ends meet. There isn't enough land, there aren't enough seeds, one year of drought and life itself is in jeopardy. There are no jobs to be had, there is no getting ahead no matter how hard she tries. The line between life and death is determined by factors well outside her control.

Walid and the other armed resistance fighters I met in the West Bank couldn't recite the data on the wealth of Palestinians. They didn't know the relative disparity between the Israelis and themselves, at least as reported by the United Nations. But they felt it. They lived it. National data reflect averages, and averages take into account both the wealthy of a country and the poor. The thing about averages in data is that few people are precisely at those averages, and Walid and his band were below it. Walid knew that he was poor in a poor country. Those young men I met recited for me both what they had—which was meager—and what they didn't have. That is, how they compared themselves with others. Much of what they didn't have was political and economic rights; much of what they did have was humiliation, confiscations, and assassinations.

I understood a little bit their sense of humiliation by the occupation. I went through the checkpoints, the wall, and the intimation of betrayal because I was "going to the other side," as the customs officer phrased it. Checkpoints within Palestinian lands, checkpoints that permitted the intrusion in areas not even near Jewish settlements. The people on the service taxi fretting as the checkpoint process begins. The disquiet of the Israeli soldiers that I would be on the service taxi with these people. The special license plates for the Palestinians, the green identity cards, the inability to enter Jerusalem, the inability to have choice. It was grinding even in my short stay in the Land.

There is an idea, prevalent in the United States, that poverty is the result of laziness, a lack of a solid work ethic. That hard work can get a person out of poverty. This is not the kind of poverty that leads to civil war. A person who is too lazy or unmotivated to look for work is unlikely to choose the rigorous life of a rebel soldier. It is when the motivated person can't get out of poverty that the problems of instability become evident. The motivated person kept down by the structure of the system in which he lives can be a dangerous person from the perspective of that system. This is the person who might make the choice to join a rebellion. This is Walid and the others with him. Articulate, bright eyes, sharp features, spoke enough English that my translator wasn't always necessary. And intense in a way that was both endearing and frightening. From his opponents' perspective, he must be frightening.

What we call structural poverty is often linked to a common pattern of identity. This is what is experienced by the landless peasant in Central America, the Karen in Burma, the Palestinian in the territories occupied by Israel, the Catholic in Northern Ireland, the Tamil in Sri Lanka, or the Chittagong Hill Tract people in Bangladesh. This is when a man will see "his people" as the first to suffer from a downturn in the economy, where the Catholic in Northern Ireland will lose his job before the Protestant does, where the Palestinian will live and die in a ghetto and the Israeli will have an apartment, where the black man in South Africa or even the United States will not, as a matter of course, have the same education, the same healthcare, the same ability to generate wealth as the white man.

Just before Christmas of 2006 I met with a Catholic archbishop of Palestinian origins living in Israel. He described this structural discrimination to me with anger and frustration just seeping from his robes. He was born in Palestine and his village was destroyed by the Israelis in 1948. With the destruction came the humiliation that continues to this day. He said to me that he can return to his village in death but not in life. The Israelis will allow the former residents to be buried in the village from which they were displaced, but will not allow them to live there. The houses remain in ruins, and the bishop remains shut out, as do they all. Although he lives a life of comfort befitting his stature in the Catholic hierarchy, his driver's license number starts with a different set of numbers than does that of a Jew. Palestinians living in Israel must renew their licenses on a specific day of the month, whereas a Jew can renew on any day he chooses. To the bishop this is a form of apartheid akin to that foisted upon the blacks of South Africa. He seethed with anger. This, a man of peace known for his counsel of forgiveness. His is a structurally imposed frustration, a form of humiliation that even a life of comfort cannot erase. When I asked him why as a young man he chose not to take up arms against the Israelis, his reply was that it was futile, that violence begets more violence, after all. Although the depth of the bishop's anger matched that of the young men behind the wall, the bishop had a way out of the most acute forms of desperation, and he had a faith that provided a spiritual release. The choices for Walid and those other young men seemed much narrower, their sense of hope much more distant. Walid is the stuff of civil wars.

Sometimes, factors conspire to leave reasonably well-off people poor. In 1986, on the border between Nicaragua and Honduras in the town of Danlí, I passed a heavily guarded refugee camp. I decided to try to get into that camp. To find somebody who might show me how, I sat on the curb outside my dumpy hotel room. This method, though odd, had worked everywhere else I had traveled in the world. Curious people approach and strike up conversations. It didn't work this time. I was a white American sitting on a street corner in a small town in Honduras, not too far from the front lines of the Nicaraguan civil war. What else could I be but CIA? Later that night, I heard that distinctive sound of live acoustic guitars coming from the building across the street. I followed the music and found a crowd of young people playing and singing. I walked in and sat down in the middle of the room, with a whole lot of curious faces staring at me. Not many words were exchanged, then one of the guitarists handed me his instrument. My rendition of "Duncan," my talent, or lack of it made me some friends by the end of that night. In the morning I was on my way into the refugee camp. I was driven up to a spot in the perimeter fencing at the far end of the camp, and with my interpreter I went through a hole in the fence. We stayed near the outer extremes of the camp to avoid detection, and I went from tent to tent talking to the people about their lives in Nicaragua, their motivations for leaving their homes for the life of a refugee, and their expectations for the future. Many of the young, the parents told me, were with the Contra army. My questions revolved around the reasons that made them leave their livelihoods in their country, send their sons out to risk their lives, and end up there, in a tent in a refugee camp. I could not imagine taking to the countryside to fight my government. The thought seemed almost ridiculous. But forces well beyond what I could comprehend at the time had compelled these people to make the choice they had.

In the 1930s, the "Okies" of Oklahoma were ravaged by the vagaries of the weather and the insensitivity of big business. What the Dust Bowl made difficult the banks made impossible, and the combined pressure caused thousands of proud farmers who had worked a plot of land for generations to migrate. Entire communities moved out as banks repossessed land that could not be made productive because of a drought. Some of the most distraught took up a gun. Most of them moved with the human wave in search of a job and a new place to live. Most ended up in refugee camps on the road to California. That was a form of structural poverty. It didn't lead to an armed insurrection, but events created the conditions that often do.

This is one of the confounding things about civil wars. Poverty is common, and civil wars are much less so. Twenty percent of the countries in the world have an annual income per person of less than five hundred dollars. Some even less than that. And yet, less than 10 percent of the countries have armed insurgencies in any one year. But it is poor countries that are more likely to have civil wars than rich ones. It takes, after all, a large number of people to make up an army large enough to challenge a government. And in a poor country, there are just more people willing to join up.

Given a grievance, given a leader, given a direction, an individual may or may not choose to take the step to sign up with a rebel army. Given that this is an act of sedition, and because there are very few ways to get out of a rebel army—victory, a negotiated settlement that includes amnesty, or death, either from a firing squad as punishment for sedition or a bullet in the heart while fighting—it is surprising that so many do sign up. It is surprising that rebel armies form, that so many countries actually end up in civil wars. And yet we know that they do. At any given point in time, there is a civil war raging in some part of the world; there are individuals who chose, for one reason or another, to be part of that war. And some form of poverty is at the root.

If we accept the basic argument that poverty—of the economic, political, or social variety—lies at the foundation of most civil wars, then there are questions about the specific mechanisms by which they play out. Evidence must join the argument to make the case that it is those who seek relief from the marginalization that comes with poverty who sign up to fight with a rebel army. The best place to look for the roots of civil war is within the struggles to survive and the structural conditions that impose them on specific groups of people. In the end not all poor countries will be caught up in the throes of civil war, and not all civil wars will be in the poorest of countries. But if I were to offer the chance to identify the next government to be challenged by armed rebellion in return for a large prize, the best money would choose from amongst the poor.

When I left Quilali, I had asked myself a question that I would attempt to answer for the next twenty years: What are the conditions under which civil wars begin and end? Without being able to fully articulate it at the time, I had stumbled across the motivations that are at the heart of civil wars: poverty and economic disadvantage. Today, nearly two decades after Nicaragua, many old civil wars still rage or simmer, many new ones have begun, all have ruined countries and taken lives by the thousands, hundreds of thousands. Many more countries will face the brutality and devastation of these wars. Civil wars are surely still in our future if this perpetual deprivation, this misery of so many lives, is not dealt with, and if the world community does not work toward change.

It is not easy to understand the motivations of people in situations so different from one's own, or to imagine what they must feel, why they do what they do. But what is impossible to ignore are the data that research has produced, the evidence that points to the reality. That poverty, a lifetime of hardship and deprivation, the humiliation that comes with discrimination, the resentment that sooner or later arises from inequality and injustice—these are fertile grounds in which the seeds of revolt will bring forth the bitter harvest of civil war. When I asked the bishop in Israel what he says to young Palestinians frustrated at their plight, he told me that he can only teach about the conditions that they face. He then reminded me that I would be much more likely to find the people who choose the violent route to change in the squalid refugee camps of the West Bank than in his town within Israel. Even though discriminated against, those Palestinians in Israel, he said, had far too much to lose. Those in the camps have simply run out of hope. I was on my way to meet the group that included Walid.

Before I take the path of evidence to understand argument, I need to go back to the struggles we face with global poverty. It might be that we can rationalize away a civil war in the Philippines or Rwanda, because the conditions those people face are so far removed from the actions we take. The dilemma of global poverty is not about me, after all, you might think, but rather about the leadership in those countries. However, food riots or revolts that result from IMF-imposed structural adjustment programs do have a link back to our wealth. But even if it is not about policy or a global economic system, it is about people. Some part of our role as world citizens is to consider the well-being of our fellow human beings. From my vantage point there is something risky, and even wrong, about pursuing my wealth at the expense of others. It is all about how we define our neighborhood. Poverty is a global scourge, with global roots and global consequences. The way I think about the world, poverty in Sierra Leone affects us in the United States. I want you to think about this global condition from a private perspective.

3

◆ ◆ ◆

FOREWARNINGS

I learned about poverty not in India or China or Ethiopia, but in Detroit, personally, as a young adult. There were years of not enough, not enough food, not enough heat, not enough of many of the things my friends had. There were five of us, raised by our father, living in a small two-bedroom house. There was no car, no phone, and sometimes little or no food. At times the family dog would be so weak that her legs wobbled. A piece of bread with butter and sugar was the afternoon fare for dog and siblings alike. Food stamps and social security were the lifeline to at least getting up in the morning and going to school. But even the social security checks went mostly for the bottles of wine that sustained my father's addiction. For a whole year the electric frying pan was used for cooking and for heating the water to bathe in. Poverty, as it turns out, can be a strange motivator.

I didn't live the life of the underprivileged youth because of structural conditions imposed by my community or government. I was born to white, college-educated parents. But I had the misfortune of having a mother die young and a father climb into a bottle of whiskey for the next decade. These were not structural conditions but situational ones. There was nobody to blame but my father. I understood the pain but did not have recourse to a method of change. From one perspective I was lucky. The only thing required to overcome my position was a change in my personal situation. That came with age, sobriety, endurance. This way out is not available for most of the impoverished of the world. Their political and social structure makes their options much tighter, their circumstances much more difficult to overcome.

The difference between structural poverty and poverty that is determined by an individual's situation is profound. Structural poverty is what the name suggests: a structure—a set of laws and regulations and the legal requirements for making them—built to generate social, political, and usually economic impoverishment. A choice made, and the result maintained, through generations by the political and economic elite. By the politically powerful. Slavery, separate but equal, voting restrictions, all targeted at one group of people, generated a set of structural conditions and a Congress that upheld these laws, laws that perpetuated the impoverishment of blacks in the United States. This happens all over the world. One of the risky aspects of structural conditions that cause poverty is that the targeted groups are homogeneous and their numbers can be large. In my family there were only five of us, and our situation wasn't the result of a choice against which we could rebel. Bad luck, bad health, and poor timing mattered most. We got older, someone put a cork in the whiskey bottle, the situation changed. Structural poverty is an entirely different matter.

On Christmas Eve of 2001 the *New York Times* ran a story about food riots in Argentina. The riots had forced the president to resign in the face of widespread opposition and the potential for mass violence. The explanation for the riots rested on economic changes instituted by the government to make the country "more efficient and competitive on the world markets." Prior to the reforms "residents work[ed] in nearby factories, and earned a decent wage ... [but] in the last few years ... those same people have been pushed into poverty." The *Times* presented a dire picture of previously self-sufficient people reduced to scavenging the garbage in order to survive. The paper quoted people who blamed the government, saying "the government created this situation, not the ordinary people, but the [ordinary] people are suffering." The working class suffered long before the middle class began to feel the squeeze. When it finally reached the middle class, the government was forced to resign.

European immigration since the 1500s influences every aspect of Argentinean life, from the food and music to the look and feel of the urban centers, the architecture and city planning, making this country the most European in South America. Lunfardo, the language of Argentine Tango and the street slang of Buenos Aires, has its roots in Italian, Portuguese, and Spanish. Buenos Aires is thought of as Rome, Paris, and London in one, and once boasted a standard of living comparable with many of the advanced countries of Europe. Since the war to Britain in 1982 over the Falkland Islands and the subsequent collapse of the military regime in Argentina, the country has had democratic government. But rampant corruption, added to a series of bad economic decisions, cheap imports, globalization, and bad advice from the IMF over the following two decades, brought the country to its knees. By 2001, foreign investors left, citizens began to convert their pesos into dollars, and the government, in dire straits and cornered by inflation and recession, defaulted on its enormous debt and faced the understandable public anger of its citizens. The historic Plaza de Mayo in Buenos Aires, where Evita Perón held demonstrations that led to the release of Juan Perón, where the military had once bombed demonstrators, where the Mothers of the Disappeared first gathered in their collective anguish over loved ones lost to military brutality, was again the site of tragedy.

What drove the people of Argentina to the brink of civil war? The simple answer is poverty. That two-year grind during which the government tried to advance its economic fortunes at the expense of working-class concessions was enough to compel normal people to make choices that they otherwise wouldn't have. Middle-class working people were now reduced to scrounging in garbage for food, and malnutrition had become rampant in once stable farm communities. The indignity of urban and rural poverty faced by a people who had lived in material and cultural prosperity, the anger of a people betrayed by their government, forced action. In effect, structural changes to the economic infrastructure that affected those living closer to the margins set the process in motion. Two years brought the situation to the breaking point. Part of the brutality of poverty is that people at the margins are at much higher risk of being drastically affected by small changes.

For those in the social sciences the resort to data is critical. We require evidence that confirms an argument before we can move forward. There are two broad types of evidence: that which describes a specific case, and that which looks for broad trends across all countries. These two types of evidence allow us to draw different types of inferences. Not necessarily better or worse, just different. What one masks the other helps uncover. The similarities across countries in strife are much greater than their differences, so broad data paint a more complete picture than any one case can give. Argentina's struggle is an example. The efficiencies sought by the Argentine government were of the same type as those advocated by the World Bank and the IMF. Cut subsidies, reduce government payrolls, open markets to external competition. Under the auspices of the Western democracies these policies are pushed on many of the poorer countries.

The question is, who gets hit hardest by reductions in government subsidies and in civil service jobs, when cooking oil becomes too expensive and public transportation curtailed? It is those at the lower end of the income scale. It is the peasants who need cooking oil, it is the villager who lacks transportation and so relies on the bus, it is the inner-city dweller who is trying to raise a young family on a modest government salary. These types of government programs are often what hold the fabric of a society together. The wealthy often pay for them, but do not need the subsidies. The poor require them for subsistence. But subsidies might not be very good for the global marketplace, at least from one economic vantage point. A more restrictive economy will promote locally produced goods to the exclusion of imported ones. Locally produced goods provide local jobs, but might not have the economies of scale of mass-produced products from a foreign country. In Argentina it took two years of pursuit of economic efficiencies to drive the pain all the way up to the middle class. The president of Argentina was smart to resign. Some political leaders choose to repress those who advocate more humane policy. That is when our dilemma of poverty begins to put at risk political stability. Civil wars are often right behind.

An economic squeeze on a group of people is taking place today in the western region of Sudan—Darfur. Sudan is the largest country in Africa. The capital, Khartoum, stands at the confluence of the Blue Nile and the White Nile. As the Libyan desert creeps into the pasturelands of the west, there is increasing competition over the scarce and dwindling resources of water and arable land, creating a situation of tension that has now escalated, encouraged by the government in Khartoum, into what has been called the world's worst humanitarian crisis. There is oil in the area, which makes it perhaps in the government's interest to further foment tensions and drive the populations out of the area, giving the government control of it. The lives of these men, women, and children, millions of them living hard lives to start with, are forever changed by the conflict, which will only get worse before it gets better, and even then probably too late for them.

To make this poverty link concrete I am going to rely on data across all countries in the world, and draw out the similarities among countries that face the threat of civil war. I take this route because it is more consistent with the type of arguments I have made, and will point to the ways that poverty is at the core of civil wars. Two sources of data will provide the primary description of the relationship between poverty and civil war. The first is data on the economic performance of countries provided by the United Nations. The second is civil war data generated in a university setting.

The evidence will rely on country averages, but country averages mask issues of distribution. In general, however, the poorer the country, the poorer the individual in that country. Though I rely on data about the average person, individuals matter. In Palestine I was told that two brothers might make different choices in their struggle against the occupation. One may join the armed resistance, the other a nonviolent organization. Individual choice was the only explanation that was offered. A few young men said that they just didn't feel comfortable with a gun, some that they were afraid of being assassinated, others that the psychology of armed struggle didn't fit their personality. It was never clear to me whether these were excuses or forms of obfuscation to make sure that I didn't think they were members of the Palestinian Resistance Committees. Whatever their motive and whatever the truth behind their stories, choosing to take up arms is a risky choice, and one that in most cases is made by the individual. The broad national data provide us a look at which countries are more likely to have large pools of young people for whom that choice seems to be viable.

An organization within the United Nations—the United Nations Development Program (UNDP)—collects data on various social and economic aspects of countries around the world. These data are useful for understanding where antipoverty programs, educational efforts, and the like should be targeted. The range of the data it collects is vast, covering the health of children, literacy, women's economic and social access, national wealth and its distribution. Not all countries provide the necessary data on all indicators, but the data are remarkably comprehensive given the diverse range of countries from which they are collected. Importantly, the UNDP also ranks countries on an index of human development, so we can get a sense of which countries are doing best and which worst, which are progressing over time and which are falling behind. These data give us a look at which countries are poor and which are wealthy, which have track records of economic decline and which have consistent economic growth. They also help point toward countries that are more at risk of civil war. I have included a table of select UNDP data at the end of the book.

Uppsala University in Sweden and the Peace Research Institute of Oslo, Norway, collect data on conflicts around the world. These data include armed conflicts within countries, and they pick up any instances of fighting that resulted in at least twenty-five fatalities. Conflict data such as these are used by researchers to study the causes and implications of conflict across a broad swath of countries and years. To make my point I'm going to focus on the data for one year, 2002, for civil wars. The year 2002 is not a special one, just close enough to today to feel "real" yet distant enough to provide reliable data.

In 2002 there were twenty-two governments confronting an insurgency in which at least twenty-five people were killed. Most of these civil wars actually resulted in at least a thousand people being killed, but a few of them were minor conflicts rather than full-blown civil wars. If these data were from 2007, Iraq would be right in there. Civil wars start somewhere, and we are not really sure of how soon killing twenty-five people in combat turns into a conflict with hundreds or thousands of fatalities. Sometimes the number of people killed in a battle is related to the vagaries of misfired weapons, misplaced bombs, or random luck. So while there is a difference between a conflict that kills a thousand people a year and one that kills only twenty-five or fifty, the explanation for these differences is not always in the intentions of the combatants. In any case, to get on the list, a country has to have an armed opposition and there must have been at least twenty-five combat-related fatalities. A conflict with twenty-five battle fatalities gives us an indication, at least, of which countries have rebel movements operating within them. The existence of armed rebel movements within a country means that there are at least two competing centers of authority, the government and any other group that has the weapons to enforce its rules over at least some people in some part of the country. From a government's point of view, twenty-five people killed in battle against the military poses a serious problem that it needs to confront.

If poverty is key to understanding when there is sufficient motivation for people to take up arms, then what we would look for is a strong relationship among indicators that reflect poor countries, poor people within countries, and the outbreak of civil war. The link at the general level requires a leap of logic, from the country to the individual. If all individuals chose not to rebel, there would be no civil war. The only ones with the guns would be the governments, and they would likely continue with their policies that lead to disgruntlement. I know from looking around the world, and from trips to Palestine, Nicaragua, and Northern Ireland, that individuals do choose to fight oppression. The data can only point to how many disgruntled people there might be, not which ones choose the path of armed struggle. So to get a grasp of which countries are most vulnerable we have to make the leap of logic.

To calculate the average income, for example, the total of the income earned within a country has to be divided by the number of people eligible to earn an income. According to the U.S. Department of Commerce the average income in the United States was $31,000 in the year 2002. A waitress working in a diner in Orwell, Ohio, does not earn that average. And neither does Bill Gates fall into that average. The number of people who earn a whole lot more than that—say a million dollars a year—is far smaller than the number who live at the poverty line. According to the U.S. Census Bureau, in 2001 about 17 million households made less than $15,000 in income, while fewer than two million made over $200,000. Many more people live below the poverty line than make over $150,000 a year. This is a question of distribution, but on "average" an American makes about $31,000 a year, at least in 2002.

In the summer of 2006, I took a bicycle trip from my hometown across New York on my way to St. Louis, Missouri. Passing through upstate New York, the poorness of that part of the state amazed me. There were trailer homes everywhere, whole towns nearly abandoned with closed stores everywhere. Globalization simply hasn't caught up with these towns; perhaps it has even impoverished them. I wondered where the young were, and concluded they were probably no longer in the town. There seemed to be no prospects for jobs, no prospects for security, probably no prospects for long-term friends. You'd just grow old in a town that grows old around you. Not quite Quilali, Nicaragua, but it made me wonder if some of the young people missing from those towns were not out fighting a war. Many of the people who remained were probably part of the wage earners in 2001 who, according to the U.S. Census Bureau, made less than $15,000.

The average tells us an awful lot about the wealth in a country, but it also masks a lot. In general, however, poorer countries—those with a lower per capita GDP—will have many more people living on the margins, they will have a much weaker social security net, and their governments will have far fewer resources with which to address the demands of those who are aggrieved. It is easy for the United States or Germany to make sure that the less well-off are not destitute, but it is much harder for Bangladesh, Sudan, or the Philippines to do so.

Today there are about 200 countries in the world. They range from very large and wealthy ones, such as the United States, France, and Germany, to small and poor countries, such as Burundi,

Togo, and Madagascar. The UNDP has information on 177 of these countries from which to develop its report. Remarkably, in 2002 forty-seven countries had per capita income levels below $500 per year. A considerable number of them have average incomes below $200 per year. We know that per capita income does not tell us anything about how equitably a country's wealth is distributed. What it does is give an indication of the depth of a country's resources, and it is the resources of a country that can be used to prevent the conditions that lead to rebellion. For example, Kuwait has a per capita income of about $16,000. This ranks the country twenty-fourth in the world in GDP. But Kuwait still has a large number of citizens living at quite low levels, and the Human Development Index ranks them only forty-fourth in the world. Kuwait generates considerable wealth through its oil resources, but the elite of the country—those tied to the royal family—take a large share of the money. In fact Kuwait does not even report the data on the distribution of its wealth. This is true of most of the oil-producing countries of the Gulf region. I can only speculate as to why, but it is probably because the distribution is dramatically skewed toward the sheiks and other members of the royal families. No political leader would want to publicize that fact. What this means is that there are poor Kuwaitis, Saudis, Americans, and Burundis, but on average there are more poor people in countries with less national wealth. Per capita GDP is just one way to get a handle on national wealth.

I have long struggled to bridge the gap between two competing bits of data about poverty and civil war. On the one hand, there are many very poor countries, and most are not facing an armed insurgency. On the other, so much of the evidence points to national income as the single best predictor of civil war. Why aren't the rest of the impoverished people of the world rising up? One of the things that is difficult is to move our thinking from a national level to that of the individual making the choice to take up arms. I was reminded of many things while sitting in a smoke-filled room with three armed members of the Palestinian resistance. The lessons are important for thinking about poverty, wealth, and the motivation to take up arms.

We met in a small room of a building just off a road that went through a Palestinian refugee camp. The meeting was arranged by two former members of the armed resistance, both of whom had spent time in Israeli prisons. To say that I was nervous would be an understatement. Part of me couldn't believe what I was doing, the other part thrilled at the opportunity to talk with people who have chosen the side of armed struggle. The streets of the refugee camp teemed with children, people sitting on stoops, laundry hanging from railings, the old and young commingled in a strange type of squalor. This was not a place where the average person would choose to live, but it was the "camp" where both of my guides grew up, and the one to which their parents came when displaced from their villages in Israel. It took about five minutes from the time we knocked on the door until we were let in the room, and for that period I stood on the street wondering whether I had made an overly risky choice. For those few minutes there was no place to run but many thoughts of doing so.

Our host was a man of twenty-nine with a big frame, close-cropped hair, and a big easy smile. There was a handgun and two extra clips on his belt, and he smoked constantly and worked the prayer beads like it was his last day. It wasn't clear to me that others would show up, so we just started talking, through my translator, about life on the run, life always with a gun. A life, he said, born of frustration and humiliation at the hands of the Israeli occupation. Before others arrived he showed me the scars of two bullet wounds from earlier confrontations with Israeli soldiers, one entering just above the heart and exiting out his back, the other through his arm. The mere thought of being in a room with someone who was armed, and had wounds to prove his prowess, was anxiety inducing, to put it mildly. It was a weird setting but Walid put me at ease right from the start. The door to the street was made of solid steel and had six big bolts that went into the frame, a door that would not be easy to kick in. Even though I was a bit shocked by the need for those bolts, I was relieved that they were there.

Over the next ten minutes two more armed men showed up, one the leader of the local cell of the al-Aqsa Martyrs' Brigades, the other a member of the Islamic Jihad. Both were armed. One had a horrific bullet wound from an earlier encounter with the Israelis, an encounter that took place when he was ten.

Two themes kept recurring through our extensive conversation. One was the lack of hope for the future, or as Professor James Fearon has described this, low expectations that things will get better. Each time I pressed them to explain their choice for the armed struggle, they would shrug with their palms up and say, "What do we have to look forward to?" The other theme was that of a common cause, a common abuse, a common struggle. In response to any question about risk or consequences, each of these men would describe the "martyrs" who had fallen before them, the abuse of their family and friends by Israeli soldiers, and the collective punishment meted out for one person's actions. In effect, they joined the armed struggle because of group dynamics. Life in the refugee camp put them into the position, but group dynamics, group identity, collective suffering made the way easy for them. As Walid phrased things, "Life is expensive as an armed fighter, but it is cheap compared to the cost of his dignity and that of the Palestinian people." The costs are high, but not high enough to overcome the cost of the loss of hope and continual humiliation. In such conditions joining an armed movement becomes normal.

When I was trying to arrange a meeting with resistance fighters, there were two responses from those who were trying to help me. The first was that the fighters would refuse because it was too risky for them. We talked about wearing masks, tying up my hands, but they said, "There are too many collaborators with the Israelis." The other reason nobody would help me arrange this was that if the resistance fighters got caught, the person who helped me set up the meeting would get killed in response. Even though everyone I met supported in principle the armed struggle, everybody was afraid of helping with arrangements. But in the process of trying to make the arrangements, the message I always got was that I would have to find these armed fighters in the refugee camps. Those outside the camps suffer from the humiliation of the occupation, but they have too much to lose. Those in the camps are poor and have little hope beyond that offered by the relief organizations. Getting into the camps seemed to be a bit like joining a club. A club of the poorest, the most abused, and those with the least hope. Not a club that the average person in a Western democracy would want to join.

This brings it all back to the central dilemma of global poverty in a time of plenty. If the only places that I could find armed resistance fighters were in the hovels and ghettoes of the refugee camps, then poverty is not only exploitive, it is destabilizing. The problems it causes us lie in the instability that becomes endemic; the core questions lie in the moral imperatives of poverty amongst wealth. As a nation, as a people, and as members of a global village, this may be the next great challenge in the evolution of human society.

If poor countries are more at risk of civil war than rich countries, we would expect more of the wars to take place in these forty-seven countries with incomes at the lower end of the income distribution. This is just what we find. Of those forty-seven countries identified by the United Nations as having per capita income below $500 per year, about one-third fought an armed insurgency in 2002. Eight countries that faced an armed insurrection in 2002 are considerably wealthier than those in the lowest category of income, though three of them had per capita incomes below $1,000 per year. Israel, Russia, and Turkey are each reasonably affluent countries, and each government faced an organized challenge from an armed opposition. Israel's case is a bit different because it has elements that go beyond a civil war and are more akin to an anticolonial struggle. But to turn this data around, 66 percent of the countries caught up in a civil war have per capita incomes under $500 per year. That tells us something about poverty and civil war (see figure).

There are two ways to think about these data. One way is that most of the civil wars take place in the poorest countries of the world and therefore poverty provides a convincing explanation for why people rise up against their governments. The other is that the majority of countries where poverty reigns are not in the throes of a civil war, at least in 2002. Poverty alone is clearly not enough to get individuals to choose violent rebellion in response to their current conditions, but it certainly seems to be an important element in the process. The poorest of the world's countries are at a considerably higher risk of a civil war than, say, the United States, France, or Germany, but something in these developed countries impedes the poor

Poverty and Civil Conflict

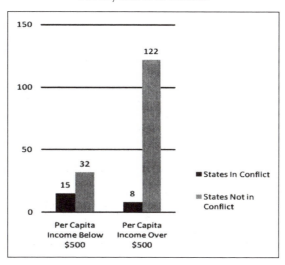

from rising up on a regular basis. Even though Walid and his band of fighters were armed in response to the Israeli occupation, the Israelis are incredibly accomplished at suppressing the armed resistance, so we don't see much of what looks like a rebel army. Those living in the refugee camps are poor, but their ability to mobilize is weak. Poverty, in this sense, might provide the motivation, but it does not provide the mechanism for the individual to take up arms. Absolute levels of national wealth are only the first step in a complex chain of events and conditions that might lead to war.

If it were just economic poverty that caused civil wars, then we would have observed at least forty-seven civil wars in the year 2002. In fact there were only about half that many, and a number of those were in the more affluent countries. The most impoverished might have the strongest motivations to change the system in which they are mired, but they also have the fewest ways to do so. It is not easy to start a rebel army, and it is unlikely that the local peasant has the contacts to organize and equip a group of soldiers. Governments in poor countries are also constrained in their efforts to prevent an insurgency. They have fewer resources with which to concede to the demands of their opponents, and they are less able to penetrate into some of the far reaches of their countries, allowing a budding rebel movement sanctuary for the short term. This combination of motivations and constraints is part of the reason that the data provide a mixed picture.

Civil wars result from a convergence of factors that come to a head at what might seem like a random point in time. Individuals have to be motivated to take extremely risky steps, groups of people who are more or less motivated to take these risks have to coalesce, and the process of trying to resolve the problems nonviolently has to break down.

Concerns over economic distress and poverty—the misery and desperation of life at the margins—can provide the individual the motivation to rebel, but there are many ways to be poor and to be squeezed. Those other eight countries at war with per capita incomes above $500 a year provide examples of this. For instance, if we look a bit more closely at Russia, Turkey, and Israel—three of those eight countries—we see that each has a particular group that is being squeezed within an otherwise wealthy and stable country. The Kurds in Turkey, the Chechens in Russia, and the Palestinians in the territories occupied by Israel are each considerably poorer than the broader population that surrounds them. Each is discriminated against politically, economically, and socially, and each forms a group that is the target for discrimination. Poverty amidst wealth can provide a motivating force. If a group creates a structure that helps make them rich and another group poor, then the expectation should not be one of calm harmony.

Being poor isn't a condition that is seen equally by all. But a great disparity in wealth is readily observable, particularly to those who are on the poor side of the street. If people are continually prevented from achieving the level to which they aspire, always kept at the bottom in spite of their desire to move up, they will blame the system that holds them down; they might prefer to change or even destroy that system.

4

♦ ♦ ♦

HOUSES BUILT ON SAND

There are places in the poorest countries of the world where steel and glass high-rises grow out of fields of slums, where mansions hide in compounds with glass-studded walls to separate them from the barrios and shantytowns. Both sides of the divide live eye to eye, nose to nose, with each other. These parallel universes are visible even in the wealthier countries; you just have to look a little harder to see them. The homeless and the chauffeured limousines use the same streets. The contrasts can be mentally deafening.

Twenty years ago in the streets of Calcutta I saw entire families sleeping in the shadows of the glass-walled office complexes. A city block served as the bedroom for untold numbers of people. In the morning a twig and some standing water were instruments for brushing their teeth; the curb was the toilet. I had traveled to Calcutta, in part, to see what life at the low end of the social hierarchy was like. With significant variation in form but not substance, the homeless sleep under the overpasses in New York City or on a subway grate in Washington, D.C. Right across the street from the Hilton Hotel in Addis Ababa is a vast slum of clapboard and corrugated tin shacks. The communal outhouse is made of the same corrugated metal, set up right next to the rusting corrugated metal fence that attempts to hide the slum from the hotel guests. It cannot hide the upscale hotel, though, from the occupants of the slum. There is probably more water in that hotel's pool than the population of that slum uses in a month, or even a year.

Even if absolute poverty is not always sufficient to motivate an individual to consider joining a rebellious movement, the level of disparity between the rich and the poor may help serve as a motivational tool. Imagine the psychological impact of living under conditions of extreme disparity. Where you beg outside the gates of the hotel and then go back to the slum with your meager take for the day. Or you are a Palestinian living in a refugee camp and see the Israelis living in the new settlement built on land confiscated from your people. Consider living in hardship, watching the wealthy living in ease. Consider always coveting what you do not have. Not all people feel this way. But it is not hard to see the potential for envy, or the incentives to rebel, that might come from watching how that other side lives. Think of the impact of knowing that the roots of this disparity go right to the structure of the relationships within a country. However the rich got rich, many others are excluded because of their race, gender, or ethnicity. This is a form of structural poverty.

Disparity in wealth is a form of poverty, but the judgment is made in terms of the disparity between the individual and the wealthy. It is about feeling poor within one country rather than being poor relative to someone in another country. This is the quintessential "haves and have-nots." We see this all the time, even in the wealthiest and most industrialized countries. The "race riots" of the 1960s in the United States pitted one group—largely blacks from the inner cities—against the authorities representing the whites who lived on the fringes of the cities or in the suburbs. The whites controlled the jobs, commerce, and dignity within the cities. The blacks looked out, excluded from the white world. The Rodney King debacle in Los Angeles in 1992 also had this flavor of the "have-nots" revolting against the "haves." Although we do see this disparity in the most industrialized countries, in the less industrialized countries the two sides of the economic distribution are in your face, palpable.

This is not restricted to having money, or not. It could be disparity in rights, disparity in access, disparity in human dignity. Take these away and there is less room for riots, and less motivation to challenge the system with the force of arms. Make them an integral part of a society, make disparities a defining characteristic, and the elite have a problem. Not an immediate one, perhaps, but one on the horizon. The list of cases where these types of systematically unequal conditions prevailed is quite long: South Africa, Rwanda, Israel, the United States, and Northern Ireland are but a few examples.

In most cases it is the wealthy who have considerably more influence within the government than do the poor. So, as any individual begins to consider the inequities to which he is bound, it would be an easy leap to link one's wealth to control of the government, and ultimately to one's own plight. Our hypothetical "normal person" might come to the conclusion that it is the wealthy who are causing him to be poor. The wealthy have been worried about this for centuries, and academics have been writing about it for generations. The shards of glass that stud the barricades are a tangible reminder that those who live behind the walls know all too well that those who live on the other side resent their wealth. Not always does this disparity lead to an armed insurgency, and in fact most of the time it doesn't. But it can contribute to the motivation that leads a disaffected individual to conclude that siding with a rebel movement is worth the risk. And this always poses a problem for the economic and political elite.

Absolute poverty and its relative cousin are, of course, linked. If you were already wealthy it would be quite unlikely that you would see the system working against you, nor would you covet your neighbor's wealth. The interaction of these two conditions only increases the motivation to take up arms. In the refugee camps of the West Bank, where the signs of a daily struggle were evident everywhere, the contrast with the villas on the hills and the Israeli settlements were stark. To get to the camps I had to take the bumps of an ill-kept road past junked cars and donkeys pulling carts. I had to drive past the Israeli settlements built on the confiscated lands that were once covered with ancient olive trees. The settlements were on the hilltops looking down and the entrance was by a nicely paved road shrouded in razor wire and security lights. There were no traffic jams on the settlement roads.

Relative disparity is difficult to identify. It is easy to see poor people but rather difficult to tell whether the poor covet the wealth or material things of the rich. Picking this up is one of those "taste and feel" experiences. If you travel across the globe it is easy to see signs of the two worlds. The disparity is more or less prevalent depending on where you are. Not everyone you ask will describe their life in terms relative to their neighbor, but some will. Twenty-five years ago I sat in a pub in Enniskillen, Northern Ireland, with a man who professed to be a member of the armed wing of the IRA. He also described for me how the Catholics got less and the Protestants got more—more and better housing, more and better jobs, better schools. He lived in a world of relative comparisons. Too many pints of Guinness later he also described the extent to which he was willing to go in the fight for independence, and who he thought were the legitimate targets in that fight. Some form of relative comparison got him in the rebel movement. I knew too well the brutality of the IRA. My grandfather cooperated with the British and became a man wanted by the IRA; they agreed in principle to allow him to come back to Ireland for the funeral of his mother, but he was wise enough not to.

The tricky part of capturing the effect of relative comparisons of disparity is that it is in each individual's head. I might be able to see clear indicators of it when I travel, but it is hard to know how individuals process it. One clear indicator that those with wealth worry about these comparisons is the extent to which they go to shelter themselves, the glass-studded walls, barbed-wire perimeters, security personnel, and the like.

Any one individual or group of people who see the system giving much more to some than they have access to is not immediately a threat to the government. This condition might help create a motivation to take action, but without some way to organize this antigovernment feeling into a group activity, these individuals are just people with a grievance against the system that perpetuates what they see as the disparity in wealth. Something that pushes this individual grievance toward a rebellion is that these disparities in wealth are often linked to disparities in political access, and quite regularly target a common group of people. People of one ethnic or religious group win from the system, people from another lose. The Shia and Sunnis in Iraq are facing this struggle today. These common conditions are kept from turning into frequent uprisings because it takes leaders to turn an individual perception of disparity into action. Someone to stand up and assume a lot of risk, someone who is willing to make demands on the government by force of arms if necessary. Such leaders are much less common than are the grievances.

When I traveled through Palestine it seemed that I was always one day behind an Israeli assassination. In Bethlehem, Ramallah, and Tul Karm I heard about the assassination of resistance fighters only the day before. The Israelis swept into Manger Square in Bethlehem to take out a cell leader one day; two days later it was Ramallah. The end to these assassinations has been a consistent demand of the Palestinians for peace negotiations. I never really understood why they were so critical to both sides of the conflict until I traveled to the Territories. The Israeli policy is designed to eliminate Palestinian leaders before they can organize a viable resistance movement. They take away those capable of leadership to prevent Palestinian ability to force the Israelis to make concessions. The Israelis arrest Palestinian political leaders whom they deem to be distasteful, but they assassinate potential military leaders. The Israelis are amazingly effective at preventing the political, social, and economic disparity from translating into an effective rebel movement. This level of anti-insurgency effectiveness does not happen in most other countries.

It requires more than just the recognition that some make more money, have more wealth, or are accorded greater opportunities to feel relatively poor. Any one individual must not only feel aggrieved by this inequality in the distribution of the wealth or opportunity, but needs also a sense that it is structurally imposed on him. In other words it is not just a notion of being on the poor end of the distribution of resources that increases the motivation to rebel, but the recognition that there is a systematic source for their misery.

The holiday food riots in Argentina in 2001 were a stark reminder that people feel disgruntled about relative disparity. According to the *Times* report, the labor class coveted the income of the middle class, who in turn viewed their condition relative to what they were just forced to give up. But the elite continued to prosper. In an environment where absolute poverty was not the norm, the perception of relative poverty was what brought the people out into the streets.

It is difficult to tell precisely when this type of relative judgment is the driving motivation behind the actions of individuals. But when I think back to the people I met in the Nicaraguan refugee camp, the overwhelming impression was that their fall from wealth and influence was traumatic. And this fall was tied clearly to policies of the government. That is, the policies were structural and targeted at specific groups within society. The people I met would not even have been poor if they had stayed in Nicaragua, but the changes in wealth that they experienced left them relatively worse off than in previous years. Trying to make the leap from a few individuals—in effect a psychological judgment by a few—to a large rebel army challenging the government is difficult, but it is made easier by examining the broad distribution of wealth within countries.

There are some ways we can use data to develop a picture of how relative disparities in wealth contribute to the motivation to join a rebel army. I'll rely again on data from the United Nations and Uppsala University. I cannot, and you should not, dismiss the intuition that lies beneath the idea that being on the short end of the distribution of the wealth can help push an individual to make that fateful decision to join a rebel army. But there are more systematic ways to draw conclusions that are supported by data from a wide range of countries. If the wealth of a country were divided equitably, then we might expect little by way of motivation to change the system that creates that distribution. We can also assume that whatever the distribution pattern is in a country, it is largely a matter of political choice. In highly unequal countries the elite are choosing to hoard wealth among the few; the structure imposes the inequity on many. Those who control the levers of government create the policies that determine the way wealth is created and distributed. Taxes, subsidies, restrictions based on race, religion, or history are the mechanisms for doing so. The less equal the distribution, the more likely the motivation to take up arms.

The importance of distributions across groups is made clear in the lifetime of research by Professor Ted Gurr. One of his pioneering efforts was to identify groups that were at risk of violence and describe how they are discriminated against. Not surprisingly there are quite a number of these groups, and some are actively involved in rebellious activities. In fact his research has identified nearly three hundred groups that have been at risk sometime during the last fifty years. Being "at risk" means that a group is in the minority within its country and is disadvantaged because of the policies of the government. According to Gurr these three hundred disadvantaged groups exist in 116 individual countries of the world. Not all of them take up arms against their government in any one year, but his research identifies the underlying potential to do so. Some groups are familiar because they are close to home, some because of recent violence. Blacks in the United States and South Africa are examples, as are Turks in Germany, Kurds in Turkey, Catholics in Northern Ireland, Palestinians in the Occupied Territories, Hindus in Pakistan, and Blacks in western Sudan.

If people are more inclined to rise up against their government when they perceive themselves to be relegated to the losing end of an unequal distribution of wealth, then we should be able to observe this trend in the data. The best way to capture this relationship between economic distribution and civil war is in terms of proportion of the wealthiest to the poorest parts of a population.

Looking at these data shows that it takes more than an unequal distribution of wealth to get a civil war, but also shows that issues of distribution are part of the problem. As a reference point I use the ratio of the income of the top 10 percent of the U.S. population to the lowest 10 percent. In 2000 it was about sixteen to one. This implies that the top 10 percent of U.S. society had sixteen times the income of the bottom 10 percent. In fact that top 10 percent of the population accounts for almost 60 percent of the wealth in the United States. By some estimates it was up to 90 percent in 2005. Think about that in terms of poverty amidst wealth. Ninety percent of all the personal wealth in the United States is held by only 10 percent of the people, while the other 90 percent of the people share just 10 percent of the wealth.

If you are in the top 10 percent of the population, this is great. But if you are in the bottom 10 percent, you are more likely to be without health insurance, less likely to be employed, less likely to have the opportunity to go to college, and more likely to be black or Hispanic. This is partially a structurally determined distribution of wealth, with the tax and incentive structures shaping the skewed distribution of wealth. The rich get richer and the poor get poorer.

Most of the wealthier countries of the world have distributions of wealth where the richest group holds about eight times the wealth of the poorest 10 percent, though the United Kingdom, Australia, and New Zealand also have double-digit ratios of rich to poor. I will use the ratio of 16:1 as a standard to judge how equitably other countries distribute their resources. This is not imposing the U.S. standard as something that is normatively justified, but it does provide a common metric for thinking about how individuals might respond to better or worse national distributions.

Of the twenty-two countries that the Uppsala data set identifies as having an armed insurgency in 2002, five have rich-to-poor ratios greater than that of the United States. Those five countries are the Philippines (16.5:1), Russia (20:1), Burundi (19:1), the Central African Republic (69:1), and Colombia (58:1). To be fair, eight of the countries with civil wars do not supply enough data for the UN to determine the ratio of distribution of wealth. If we assume that these countries have a worse distribution ratio than the United States, then more than half of the countries with skewed levels of distribution fought insurgencies in 2002. The assumption that no information is equal to a substantially unequal distribution might not be valid, but in a couple of the countries we can use intuition. The Democratic Republic of the Congo was for over twenty years ruled by a tyrant who amassed great wealth at the expense of the people of the Congo. Mobutu's thievery was so rampant that his economic policies caused his regime to be referred to as a kleptocracy. The Congo had a civil war in 2002. The Palestinian Territories occupied by Israel pose a different problem for inference, but it would be clear to most observers that the distribution of wealth between Palestinians and Israelis is dramatically skewed, even though the distribution within Israel proper is not quite so bad. As a group, however, the Palestinians have far less wealth than the Israelis. Of the data that are available, the average income of a Palestinian living in the Occupied Territories is just over U.S. $1,000 per year, while the average person living in Israel earns over $15,000 per year.

One way to check the sensitivity of the result using the United States as the standard is to relax that standard. There is nothing hard and fast about a 16:1 distribution of wealth that would set individuals on the path to civil war; it is simply a way to judge relative to a country that we know well. If I relax that standard to the level of 10:1—where the richest 10 percent have ten times the wealth of the poorest 10 percent—we see that now eight of the twenty-two countries are in the midst of a civil war in 2002, six are not, and eight other countries do not supply enough data to tell. Depending on what assumption we make about those countries that do not report enough data, we could conclude that up to 72 percent of the governments in countries with somewhat unequal distributions of wealth were confronting armed insurgencies.

How much of a disparity in wealth or income is necessary before people rise up in large numbers? There is no real hard and fast figure, and social science research has yet to provide a firm answer. It is the underlying structure that adds to the motivation. Inequity in distribution is yet another form of stress with consequences and moral implications. Combined with other forces that put the squeeze on those at the margins, the seams of society can rupture. At what point would you start to consider a violent challenge to a system that works against you? At what point would you be susceptible to the arguments of a charismatic rebel leader advocating a forceful change to the power structures? At what point would you be willing to confront your own poverty amidst extreme wealth?

To put this into perspective, examples of other countries with dramatically skewed levels of distribution are South Africa (65:1), Guatemala (55:1), Argentina (39:1), and Venezuela (63:1). So that nothing is lost in the interpretation, let me make these dramatic inequalities clear. South Africa and Guatemala just went through long periods of armed struggle, and Argentina had protests and riots in

2001 that forced the president to resign. Venezuela has recently been confronted by political instability because its elected president has adopted policies designed to redistribute wealth in that country from those who have the most to those who have less. Perhaps he learned a lesson from the past experiences of other countries. In Venezuela today it is not the poorest who are agitating, it is those threatened by the redistribution: the richest.

As with absolute levels of poverty, the distribution of wealth is an important element in whether or not a country finds itself embroiled in a civil war. But also like absolute poverty, the distribution does not explain it all. There are too many countries with levels of distribution on a par with or better than western European countries that still find themselves at war. This is as I would expect when looking for explanations for complex relationships with complex outcomes. The evidence is not perfect but it points in a common direction.

The choice to rebel is not that simple. There is reason to think that people also focus on the immediate past and their expectations for the future, rather than on how the rich people live or how desperately poor they are. In other words, for many it is easier to endure an impoverished or inequitable situation than it is to face sudden changes in their economic, political, or social fortunes. When people or the process start taking things away from you, you start taking things away from them, most importantly your support for political authority.

5

♦ ♦ ♦

TIPPING POINT

My high-school-aged son was recently struggling through Steinbeck's *The Grapes of Wrath*. To him the book is dry and boring. To me it is a great American novel. I tried to explain to him that Steinbeck uses historical fiction to describe the conditions that lead large groups of people to confront choices about life and death, revolution and starvation, humiliation and protest, one family member over another. My son is looking for action and intrigue. Steinbeck tells a story that is riveting because the event that is the backdrop of the story held the potential for yet another American rebellion. Had things played out differently my son might have been riveted by a very different version of that story. But it certainly leads back to the same question. Under what conditions would you join a rebellious movement? One of the Okies could have answered that.

When persistent drought turned the farmland of Oklahoma into a terrible place to try to eke out a living, the farmers became worried. But they had struggled through hard times for generations and they had almost always bounced back when the next string of good luck came around. So there was hope. But in the 1930s when drought pushed many at the margins over the edge, the banks were right there just waiting to foreclose on the farmers' loans. Changes in banking, changes in economies of farming, and dramatic changes in the weather forced entire communities on the road to refugee camps along the California border. The past, even though it had been hard, looked better than the prospects for the future in Oklahoma. Similar stories can be told elsewhere about the Depression era, but there are many more subtle forms of turning the future against those living at the margins.

Structural poverty has many faces. Although in any country or for any individual these conditions may change, the pace is often glacial. The rags-to-riches stories are more myth than real, and in general the landless are born into and die out of those conditions. We also know that people will not always rebel against poverty, or the relatively poor conditions that they find themselves in, and apparently most of those who are impoverished endure their hardship with grace, even if they detest their lot in life.

It is a tragic fact that almost all countries experience civil wars during some part of their political development. But they are not constants within the history of any country. People rise up against their government, and then are complacent for generations. This happens even though the country is poor, is undemocratic, or maintains a skewed distribution of wealth for the whole time. In short, changes that take place over time are at the foundation of rebel movements and civil wars. There are several factors that change within a country that can affect the motivation for a normal individual to give up that normal life in exchange for life as a rebel soldier. Some of these changing conditions are rooted in economics, some in politics.

Economic changes could be a result of government policy or the vagaries of the international system. When an economy is changing for the better, most people will be less threatened by how and how fast the changes occur. But when the change is for the worse—when the economy is contracting, for instance—fear and uncertainty can create formidable foes. Two types of economic distress can turn an economy against those living at the margins or move the working class closer to them: inflation and a chronic recession. Inflation is the annual increase in wages and prices. Sometimes these can be extreme at other times they creep up over an extended period of time. A recession is when the income of the country declines over time. Most of us have experienced a downturn in the economy without undue hardship, but when it is sustained for an extended period it can have a dramatic effect on an individual's ability to prosper, or even survive.

On my trip to Palestine, I was startled by the frequency with which I met Palestinians who had lived for years in the United States, Canada, or some other western European country. Many were citizens of those countries, and most had quit fairly lucrative jobs to return to their homeland. They had all been enticed by the possibilities resulting from promises held out by the Oslo Peace Accords. Money flowed in along with people; hotels and other projects sprang up over the West Bank. Then in September 2000, Ariel Sharon went to the Dome of the Rock, one of Islam's holiest sites, and inflamed Palestinians, who took his action as an affront to Islam and to Palestine. The years of conflict that followed dashed the hopes of Palestinians and Israelis alike, but the fall from economic and political grace has been steep for the Palestinians.

The effect of economic and political change can be dramatic. Wealth can mean different things in different cultures and to different people: stocks in the industrialized countries, land, camels, or cows in others. Individuals build up expectations over time about where they will be in the future, and they do so in part by intuitively plotting the trends of their recent past and building a mental model of their expectations. We all do this. Young people focusing on buying a house, a car, or saving for a dowry; people later in their careers focusing on retirement savings or saving for their children's education. What seems common is that our expectations are based on our financial positions up to this point. We have all heard the tragic stories of the Wall Street brokers who lost everything during the Great Depression and then took their own lives because they could not endure the crushing impact of the sudden change in their fortunes. That kind of change can be devastating to our ability to provide for ourselves and our families, to our social status, and to our egos. Depending on how someone sees the source of the problem and how it has been foisted upon them, reactions can take many forms. Those who live at the margins of survival are no less vulnerable to changes than those who have fortunes to lose. In fact those at the margins may be much more at risk from a declining national economy. Weak or weakening expectations for the future can frighten people into accepting risks that they might otherwise not consider.

Strikes, shutdowns, and lockouts are more prevalent in the United States and countries where elections tend to hold sway over rebellion. When the Spanish government puts fishing constraints on the Spanish fleet, those whose livelihoods depend on fishing take to the streets to denounce the government. Their incomes are at stake and protest is the vehicle available to them to try to create a change in government policy. Their fate is tied to structural policies implemented by the government. A persistent economic downturn in a country that does not have access to political protest, as such, can pose a significant problem for those who are harmed by the policies and whose futures are at risk. If they protest, they get abused by the government; if they try to endure their new hardships, they risk falling into the ranks of the impoverished. The individuals who make the choice between protest, rebellion, and endurance have to project out into the future to see if their expectations warrant risky actions.

One of the amazing things about the economic collapse in the Palestinian Territories is that many shoulder the burden collectively. The former middle class, which is getting hammered by the confiscation of funds by the Israelis and the virtual disappearance of tourist dollars, is falling back on family ties. Where four worked before, one might have a job today; the one supports the families of the other three. This is much harder, of course, in the refugee camps, and it is in the camps that I found the armed resistance fighters. If the economic burden continues, we could expect more from the middle class to side with the armed Resistance Committees that congregate in the refugee camps.

I spent an afternoon on the campus of a Palestinian university talking with student leaders about the conditions they face, the armed struggle, and potential solutions. After a short time the group around me began to swell. Two opinions I heard constantly throughout my visit were that opportunities were drying up, and that the armed struggle was justified in light of Israeli policies. I asked the group of students whether any of them were willing to use their talents as engineers and computer scientists to assist the armed struggle. From the crowd there was a collective rumble in Arabic that I could not understand, but I took it to be a veiled yes, at least in principle. One man talked about former students who had put their talents to work as bomb makers and such, and I got the sense that they were revered. But there was one young man who had the look—his eyes suggested to me that his answer was a much clearer yes. I singled him out and engaged him directly. It was an awkward moment because I think we both understood the implications of this private conversation within the group. The group fell silent. Through my interpreter he told me that the occupation made it hard to think about how he would use his training, that the opportunities were so constrained and the level of frustration so high that participating in the armed struggle made sense. So I took the next step and asked him if he was a member of the armed resistance. His response was subtle, but he scanned the now rather large crowd and replied to me in English that there were "too many spies and collaborators" for him to answer. My sense was that if this young man did not have other opportunities, he was going to be an active member of the armed resistance. To him his future did not look good enough, and the past does not provide him with enough reason to think otherwise. He, too, had the feel of a man from whom civil wars are made.

Without some form of economic hardship few normal people might ever consider the option of walking away from their job and home and taking up arms with a rebel army. So if you are trying to fit yourself into a situation that might compel you to take up arms against your government, think about how you value the future in relation to how you see your future prospects.

We can get a sense of future expectations and economic distress by looking at how the country is performing economically over time. Most of us are keenly aware when the economy is growing or contracting, and in fact we generally hear about it at regular intervals on the news. If you lose your job, you cannot pay your mortgage, or the lack of raises makes your financial struggle harder, you can relate to a poor economy. In the United States, presidential elections are often won or lost by whether the economy is growing, and if so, fast enough to create jobs. The economic stimulus of early 2008 and the political expediency with which the government pulled it off is a testament to the importance of economic stability. When an economy is contracting, people tend to be fired from their jobs at much faster rates than when an economy is expanding. Often economic contraction or expansion can be tied to government policy, and most governments spend considerable effort to keep their economy expanding and to prevent dramatic swings in growth or decline. When an economic contraction is sustained over a number of years, future expectations need to be revised, most often downward. People feel the pinch. The lower you are in the economic hierarchy, the more painful are the adjustments that you have to make. When those revisions and adjustments become drastic, an individual might begin to view the risks and rewards associated with rebellion as providing a better future than riding out current conditions. At this point the government has problems.

To put this into practical terms, if a government can manipulate an economy in a way that minimizes the prospects for a bleak future, it should. The policies with which to do this are often a matter of political debate. Tax cuts versus government spending, subsidies versus market forces. But sometimes the policies are a matter of private gain. Corruption reduces the amount of government resources available to make fair economic policy. One group of leaders enriching themselves at the expense of the future prospects for the rest. Many in Palestine would say that this describes the actions of the Palestinian Authority, and largely explains the political victory of Hamas in 2006. One need look no further than Mobutu in Zaire to understand how devastating government corruption can be. A corporate economic model based on a system of globalized markets can be just as exploitive as corrupt leaders pulling the reins of government, just through different mechanisms.

The data collected by the UNDP and Uppsala University provide a window on the relationship between changes in the national economy and rebellion or civil war. By focusing on those twenty-two countries facing an armed insurrection in 2002, we can look to see how many of them were also suffering from a downturn in their economies. Initially, if there were a sustained decline in an economy over time, this might lead a person to calculate that things are bad and not likely to get better anytime soon. Expectations for a turn-around, therefore, might be low. We can also look to the short term. People in economic distress or who live at the margins do not hold to a long-term horizon. I can point this out with economic growth rates in industrialized democracies that are quite familiar to most. If you listen to quarterly economic reports—particularly in the run-up to an election—three and four percentage points dominate the U.S. debate. That is, most economists and politicians see a robust rate of growth in the United States to be in the three to four percentage point range. Growth rates of less than 2 percent reflect a sluggish economy, one that is most likely shedding jobs and causing political anxieties. There have been, for instance, only four years of the last twenty-two when the U.S. economy grew at rates lower than 2 percent. An economic decline has happened in only four of the last thirty years—1975, 1980, 1982, and 1991. The apparent political consequences were stark. In 1976 Jimmy Carter beat incumbent president Gerald Ford, in 1980 Ronald Reagan beat incumbent president Jimmy Carter, and in 1992 Bill Clinton beat incumbent president George H. W. Bush. Economic downturns have real political consequences.

Over a long period of time—the quarter century between 1975 and 2002—the average rate of growth in all the wealthy industrial economies of the world has been about 2 percent per year, and over the decade of the 1990s that rate has been about 1.7 percent. If we break these data down to a few individual countries, we see that the United States averaged a growth rate of 2 percent over both periods; the United Kingdom averaged 2.1 percent and 2.4 percent, respectively; and France averaged 1.7 percent and 1.6 percent over the two periods.

To get a sense of the risk from poor economic performance I use two indicators to describe how an individual in a country might evaluate her economic fortunes. One is a sustained *decline* in an economy, measured at twenty-five years and ten years. This is a very tough standard, particularly over the longer period, because an average negative growth rate over two and a half decades would virtually eliminate economic vitality within a country. Poverty would be rampant and the ability of the government to resuscitate the economy limited. The other standard is much more lenient, comprising a *growth rate* of under *1 percent.* A sluggish economy can still perform, but in order to have a sluggish average over a couple of decades, either growth is continually anemic or there have been extended periods of considerable economic decline. Either one leaves people at the margins in a tough spot; the question is whether it is tough enough to risk taking up arms.

Think about what this means to that average individual who is trying to keep his family fed, clothed, and housed. The closer to the margins, the more difficult this is, but when an economy is contracting or anemic, the squeeze is on. The loss of a job, the loss of credit, the inability to buy seeds, the need to sell livestock cheap, or the loss of purchasing power can wreak havoc. If there is no expectation for a positive change, normal behavior may give way to desperate actions. Recruitment into a rebel army may begin to look like a viable option, even the only good one. To many who study civil wars, a job in a rebel army is just another form of labor. In a failing economy, or in a poor town, if you cannot get a job in a factory or farm, you would be more likely to take one in a rebel army.

There are poor towns all over the world, and there are poor towns down the street, and just over the next ridge. On that bicycle trip I took the summer of 2006, I rode through many such towns right here in the United States. On a bicycle the world is close around you; it isn't like driving through the country at high speed on a freeway within the insulated confines of a car. I suffered the condition of back roads, felt wind on my skin, smelled roadkill on the asphalt, ate in small restaurants, saw the trailers and the flags. I marveled at the beauty of the countryside. I found a United States I didn't know was still out there, behind the Taco Bells and giant gas station rest stops. It is there, but I found it has a tenuous existence. Those towns reminded me of other places I had been—Bangladesh, Tanzania, Ethiopia, Guatemala. I once went to Calcutta so I would understand life at the bottom of the social hierarchy, so I could keep it in mind as I lived among the affluent. This trip across upstate New York twenty years later taught me that lesson all over again.

I passed decrepit old homes that must have less value than the gear on my bicycle. They flew the American flag. Cars passed me, some that didn't look as if they would last another day; they flew the flag too. This American flag stands for all the good things in this country, freedoms, opportunities, all the things the people in these towns do not have. So many of the towns are nearly abandoned, shops held open by dint of history. And yet, the flag is everywhere. I don't believe the people living in trailers and run-down homes, working in the few remaining stores and restaurants, exercise their freedom of speech with much regularity. They don't seem to have the freedom of opportunity as determined by job prospects either. Nor do I think their option of mobility is reason for saluting the flag. Perhaps the flag represents something else entirely to the people here. Not something they did not have—the freedoms and opportunities—but something they did: it was a reminder of the military might and consequent superiority of the United States. These are the towns, after all, where the military fills its lower ranks.

These are places from where opportunity has left, and with it the aspirations of those who did not, or could not, follow it out the door. I came face-to-face with one such person one morning as I drank my morning coffee in a restaurant with hardly any customers. I was in a town in Ohio. I was looking, ironically, for the best route out of town. My waitress was little older than I. I asked her how far up Route 45 was. She said she couldn't help me with that information—she did not drive. I knew it was just a bit up the road, and said as much. She told me again she did not drive, and so didn't get up that far. She said she didn't have a car because she had to pay insurance on her house, and if she had one, she would have to pay insurance on that too. I asked about a bus station, a train. There were none. Her physical range, then, like that of so many of the working poor in Bangladesh or Ethiopia, was no more than twenty miles. She said work was scarce in those parts; she told me about a friend of hers who had returned from vacation to find she had no job. I had heard the same story from the man I rode into town with. The director of human services called him into his office one morning, and thirty minutes later he was home for good. He was fifty-eight.

My waitress advised me, if I had a job I should do as my boss told me to do. She was haunting, trapped. The cook in the restaurant was a young woman of about twenty. To me it seemed that she too wore that same mantle of hopelessness, despair. This was the ethos of mobilization. It is hard to think of in the United States. But in other countries with less secure governments and more elites willing to challenge them, these are the very people who can be mobilized for rebellion. It is from towns like these that the U.S. military recruits. The best opportunity in such towns is the chance to join the military, to kill or be killed defending the very freedoms and opportunities they cannot be part of. It was in the refugee camps in Palestine that I found the armed resistance. There, too, despair ran high and hope was gone. In countries where there are more poor people, there exists a larger pool of people who are desperate and hopeless, a larger pool available for mobilization. These are the sorts of people, whether in the United States or Nicaragua, who become fodder for armies, either government or rebel.

When looking at the data, the toughest test of the proposition—a decline over twenty-five years—accounts for almost one-quarter of all the countries involved in a civil war in 2002. That is, five countries had declines in their national income over the period between 1975 and 2002. Those five countries are Rwanda, Angola, Burundi, Algeria, and the Central African Republic. Of course some of the poorer and more violent countries have not reported the information to allow for this comparison, but most of the countries involved in internal strife experienced at least some growth in their economies in the last quarter century. But depending on how you view missing data, there was a considerable proportion of the countries fighting civil wars in 2002 that were coming off a very long string of bad economic years.

Over a shorter period of time—the decade of the 1990s—there are seven countries, one-third of the total, that fall into the sustained decline category, with Russia (–2.4 percent) and the Palestinian Territories (–4.9 percent) adding to the original five. During the 1990s Burundi's national income dropped by nearly 4 percent. If this national trend played out at the level of each individual, it would translate into a one-third reduction in income over a ten-year period. Without offsetting increases in wages the purchasing power of an individual would be 35 percent lower at the end of the decade than at its beginning. A decade gives ample time to adjust, but the change in the standard of living would be dramatic. For the person living at the margins adapting to such a sustained decline might be impossible. With no expectation that things will get better, changing the government may look appealing. Whether you look back ten or twenty-five years, a decline in income over such a long period must lead an individual to evaluate—or reevaluate—her strategy for surviving. We know that every individual is not going to experience a decline that mirrors that of his country's, but on average the poor pay a higher cost than the wealthy when economies go through wrenching times. Not only do the poor have less to fall back on than the rich, but they also occupy the jobs and the lands that are most susceptible to termination or reclamation. The safety net for those at the margins generally does not adjust for changes in inflation.

The more relaxed standard, that of a sluggish rate of growth of less than 1 percent, accounts for double the number of countries with civil wars in 2002. If we just focus on the ten confirmed cases of sluggish growth over the two and a half decades preceding 2002, these countries account for 45 percent of all the countries with civil wars in that year. To me that is quite remarkable. Over the 1990s there are nine countries with anemic growth, and two countries that sit right on the fence. The implications are quite profound and if we go back to the level of intuition, a number of things come into focus. The clearest of these is the willingness to endure poverty.

All of the evidence that we could muster—by looking around the world or around our neighborhoods—would show that people will endure harsh and impoverished conditions, sometimes for a lifetime. But even people living at the margins have aspirations, have dignity, and expect better things to come. When I worked in Mother Teresa's home for the destitute and dying in Calcutta, the most striking thing about the "patients" was how they tried to maintain their dignity in spite of extremely trying circumstances. They demanded things that I never would have thought someone on her deathbed would consider important. A good haircut, which really meant shaved very closely to the scalp; clean clothes, meaning not stained; and warm slurry that passed for soup that we fed them. Even though they would probably die the next day, they wanted to be as clean and proper as possible until their time came. They wanted to be dignified until the very end. I went there looking to find out something about how the most impoverished survive and I came away marveling at the power of human dignity.

When poverty is combined with a continual decline in the pool of resources that could help uplift the impoverished, hope diminishes. And hope diminishes not only for those at the bottom looking up, but also for those who have more and are looking down. If the hope is removed and replaced with fear, then risks become more real. The "rational peasant," the person who would normally endure hardship, begins to see the rewards of rebellion and the risks from not rebelling in a more favorable light.

It should also be clear that many of the countries caught up in a civil war in 2002 did not just come off a bad period of economic anemia or contraction; they were living it for up to a generation. Change is important, and there are a number of changes that can move a country across the threshold from peace to war, but not all involve economics. Before we go there, there is one more economic factor to take into account: inflation.

Inflation can be a grind. Under normal economic conditions you will know inflation by the small increase in the cost of things from one year to the next. If the rate of inflation is small enough, each person just works it into her budget; employers often accommodate inflation by automatic increases in wages; and we all come to accept it as part of life. But it isn't always like that.

The price of a Ford Maverick in 1972 was about $2,000; today a comparable car would probably cost well over $10,000. My parents bought their first house for $11,000; today that same little brick house is worth upwards of $100,000. The difference is in large part due to inflation. When the rate of inflation is rapid, we all take notice.

Mortgage rates skyrocket, for example, so the cost of buying a house might rise faster than the average person's ability to do so. Businesses borrow money to produce the goods that we buy, and when the price they pay to borrow goes up rapidly, they pass this cost along to us. The costs of bread, milk, lawnmowers, bikes, homes, and cars rise more rapidly than our employers can increase our wages. Unions—and individuals—demand more than employers can contribute in the short term, so strikes and other forms of labor unrest become more prevalent. All of this will happen in the United States or western Europe. The net effect of high rates of inflation is that the value of our money or wealth declines as the goods we buy cost more. During highly inflationary times most people see a downward trend in their purchasing power, their wealth, and sometimes their ability to cope with the basic necessities of life. This can be quite traumatic for those living on the margins, and as is often the case, many countries fighting civil wars are in economic dire straits.

So how much inflation is too much? The real answer is that we don't know, but if you consider two elections in the United States you should be able to see how inflation plays out in public attitudes, at least in a highly democratic and quite wealthy country. During the period January 1974 through January 1975 the rate of inflation in the United States was nearly 12 percent, and over the period January 1974 through January 1976 inflation consumed over 19 percent of the value of the U.S. dollar. It also happened that a relatively unknown politician, Jimmy Carter, beat the sitting president, Gerald Ford, for the presidency in 1976. Just four years later the problem was even worse. Ronald Reagan was challenging President Jimmy Carter for the presidency, and during the thirteen-month period from January 1979 through January 1980 the rate of inflation was 14 percent. Ronald Reagan won the election. In both elections there were many issues besides the rate of inflation that influenced the outcome of the election, but the economy certainly loomed large in people's minds and in the campaigns. As political scientists are fond of saying, people vote their pocketbooks.

What happens when inflation far exceeds the levels experienced by the United States in the late 1970s and early 1980s? Brazil, for example, had an average annual change in its consumer price index—which measures the rate of inflation—of over 130 percent per year during the 1990s! That means that the price of everything more than doubled in each year. Planning for a weekly, let alone a monthly, budget becomes impossible under these levels of inflation. The Democratic Republic of the Congo (DRC, once Zaire) had an annual rate of inflation of almost 700 percent per year during the 1990s. How do you cope when your wealth declines perceptibly on a daily basis? The first thing to do is to get your money out of the formal economy, and if you are wealthy enough, get it right out of the country. But as this withdrawal from the economy takes place, the government begins to lose legitimacy, just as former presidents Ford and Carter did in the United States. To make it worse, as individuals begin to pull out of the formal economy, the government has less room to maneuver in trying to make things better for those feeling the pinch. This is the type of economic conundrum that most political leaders would love to avoid, and it is this type of economic uncertainty that drives both the economic elite and those living at the margins to despair. The object of their despair is their expectation for the future.

Let's go back to the data for a moment. The pattern we would be interested in is how the long-term and short-term rates of inflation are associated with civil war. If inflation was high and had been so for a number of years, many of the elite would already have taken their money out of the country, and those less well-off would be looking for ways to circumvent the official economy. Over a sustained period, inflation would grind away at the legitimacy of the government, and it might be easier to convince individuals to join the rebels if their jobs were no longer sufficient to feed and house their family, and if they saw no prospect for change.

What do the data tell us? I'll look at two periods of time, the decade of the 1990s, and the year 2001, immediately prior to the year we observe civil wars. There are data on the consumer price index for nineteen of the twenty-two countries that were confronting an internal insurgency in 2002. Six countries, Russia, Burma, the

Democratic Republic of the Congo, Turkey, Indonesia, and Angola, had double-digit inflation in the period 2001 to 2002, roughly one-third of all of those at war. Inflation in any one year is not likely to be the immediate trigger that sets off an armed insurgency, unless that one year was preceded by a long string of other highly inflationary years. By the end of a decade of high inflation, individual purchasing power would be substantially reduced and expectations for the future would look grim.

When I look at the 1990s at least ten of the twenty-two countries had double-digit inflation. In real terms, this means that a person earning U.S. $10,000 in 1992 (a considerable sum for this sample of countries) would have the purchasing power of $3,500 one decade later. And after a decade of economic decline little reason to anticipate changes for the better. To make this clear, about 45 percent of the governments confronting an armed rebellion suffered from chronic inflation over the previous decade. If you are a specialist in rebel recruitment, these countries might be a good place to look! Were there countries with double-digit inflation that did not end up in a civil war in 2002? Yes. Just like all the other indicators, inflation is not necessary for a civil war, nor is it sufficient to pull a country into one. Civil wars result from a host of bad policies and complex social, political, and economic processes. The evidence seems clear, though, that many countries facing armed insurgencies also confront the scourge of inflation.

The economic motivations behind civil wars are part of a process. Individuals might look at how the structure of their political system influences their situation. Getting to a civil war is like pushing a boulder up a hill. A long, hard economic grind can help push that metaphorical boulder up the hill. If inflation or inequality or poverty is taking a very big toll, the first reaction might not be to charge the police station with a hunting rifle. In most instances an individual does not have any immediate way to turn discontent into violent antigovernment action. He could, however, go to a clandestine meeting to see what other citizens are thinking and doing. This is what rebel organizers hope for and encourage.

From the personal perspective, how much bad economic news would it take for you to act to change the policies of your government? These actions would involve extreme risks for an uncertain outcome. But given poor conditions and not much hope for change, those risks might seem worth the potential rewards.

6

♦ ♦ ♦

PERFECT STORM

My first exposure to a situation that felt like a civil war took place not in Cambodia, but later, during my travels in Bangladesh in 1983. I was exploring the countryside outside the capital city when an uprising brought the military out into the streets. Unfortunately, I had lost my passport and so was at the time an undocumented alien in a country under martial law, on the brink of upheaval. I made the journey back to Dhaka hidden under a pile of luggage in the back of a bus. I ended up confined to the tenuous safety of a local YMCA compound with a group of other foreigners. The military had set up a sandbag fortification, complete with machine guns, right outside that compound. Protesters came from the side streets to confront them, and were beaten and thrown in the back of an army truck. After that, neither I nor any of the other guests at the compound had any interest in going any further than peering over the compound wall. Seeing one protester beaten and carted away was enough to dissolve my naive thoughts of joining the dissidents. Standing at the barricade took on an entirely different meaning.

Through the next few days I witnessed several more people beaten and taken away to some unknown location in those army trucks, to be further beaten, I imagined. The military wrapped up the rebellion, and had the city back to normal within three days. From my own response to this experience, I would assume that the rational person would hunker down at home and let the event pass without personal incident. The brutality stunned and scared me, and yet, I was intrigued. Why, I thought, would people who faced such insurmountable odds challenge a military that held overwhelming power?

Even protest is dangerous in many countries, let alone armed rebellion. Armed rebellion is an act of sedition. It is unlikely, therefore, that a stagnant economy, or a few years of inflation, or poverty, however extreme, would singly suffice to motivate an average person to join an armed uprising. Sometimes, though, more than one of these economic pressures coincide, increasing the burden on an individual and a country.

Unlike poverty, which can be clearly seen, or unequal distribution, which is evident when you look across the street or into other neighborhoods, inflation and stagnation are visible in economic data rather than through observation. Life in the barrio is hard because the people there live under difficult economic conditions. In Palestine the barrio is the refugee camp in the Occupied Territories. In Ethiopia the barrio is the tin-walled enclave with hundreds of corrugated metal shacks looming just outside the tree-lined Hilton Hotel. In Guatemala City low-lying areas are consumed by tin-and-cardboard hovels, while up on the hillsides security perimeters guard big houses. Inflation and stagnation do affect both sides of the street, but not equally. As in most barrios, in the Palestinian refugee camps adult men were wandering aimlessly through the streets and alleyways. Children played with things that could hardly be described as toys. I had the feeling of far too many people crowded into far too little space. Many of them rely on foreign aid to make ends meet because that is the only option they have. It was here that I found men with guns willing to talk with me about the value of fighting for change. To an attentive observer, the existence of black market money exchange and the signs in shop windows announcing the changing value of currency or the price of bread will tell a story of underlying economic stress. But it is hard to see inflation while walking in a barrio. Economic stress is clearly visible in the indicators of life expectancy, infant mortality, and educational achievement—indicators of the basic quality of life.

Consider the evidence we have on those twenty-two countries fighting insurgencies in 2002. In half of those countries people earned below $500 annually. If earning $1,000 annually could be considered poor, then thirteen of those countries, or 60 percent of them, are poor. Annual income, then, is an important factor in the equation, but does not explain all civil wars. When we look at how wealth is distributed within the population, only five of the countries at war were worse off than the United States. Over a third of the countries do not report on distribution. It is debatable why they do not, but not a stretch to surmise that the distribution in these countries does not meet this standard.

If we look at data on the state of the economy over the twenty-five years leading up to 2002, the economy had *declined* in five of the countries at war in 2002, and ten of them had annual growth rates averaging less than 1 percent a year. This means nearly half the countries at war in 2002 had economies that were stagnant or declining over a quarter century before a civil war broke out. Also, 50 percent of all the countries involved in a civil war in 2002 had experienced double-digit rates of inflation over the previous ten years. Twenty-five or even ten years of a stagnant or declining economy would be hard to endure. If it were coupled with a decade—or even two or three years—of inflation, it would force those at the margins to survive outside the normal economy, if not at the edge of disaster.

When several different economic stresses are heaped on the same country, the individual within that country has a tough time. When the data show overlaps on these indicators of average income, distribution of wealth, and inflation, we are looking at a picture of a country that is not only poor but in long-term stagnation, even decline. This kind of long-term economic stagnation gives people little hope that bleak conditions will ever change for the better. These conditions could well provide motivation for individuals to join up with a rebel cause. I knew, for example, when I witnessed the brutal treatment of the protesters at the hands of the Bangladeshi military that their battle cry was not simply high inflation or low income. There had to be a high degree of pent-up frustration for them to confront what was certainly going to happen to them.

By focusing on the six indicators explored in the earlier chapters, it is clear that of those twenty-two countries involved in civil war in 2002, none of them were on the good side of all of the indicators. An exception is Israel, only if you exclude data reported on the Occupied Territories. But since the fighting is over the Territories, there seems little reason to exclude those data. In fact, these data from Israel and the Occupied Territories gives us one of the few instances where we can compare across the groups at war, something I will take up in the next chapter. But four countries of those twenty-two do poorly in only one category. This tells us that a country doesn't have to be an economic basket case to find itself embroiled in a civil war. But many of those governments fighting insurgencies do preside over these economic basket cases, where poverty is rampant, growth anemic, and hopes for the future dim.

Burundi was clearly below the threshold on five of the six indicators, and at least ten countries had a poor showing on three of the six indicators: the Congo, Angola, Chad, Russia, Rwanda, Algeria, Sudan, Colombia, Burundi, and the Central African Republic. Seven countries fell below thresholds on at least four of the indicators and yet were not at war in the year 2002. But these seven are certainly not a collection of the most peaceful countries in the world. In fact these countries have been unstable or violent in the recent past, and seem destined to be in the future. For instance, Sierra Leone, Guinea-Bissau, and Haiti have recently gone through periods of internal conflict that puts them in Uppsala's data set, just not in 2002. Zambia and Madagascar also fail the test of the economic indicators that point to economic stress, but they have been relatively peaceful in recent times. Nigeria is inching its way toward a civil war, and only a generation ago fought a bloody war over Biafra. The easy inference to draw is that poverty and economic distress in combination increase the motivation for people to take up arms against their government.

There are other ways to explore how people make what may be the riskiest choice of their lives. Indicators such as infant mortality rates, spending on education, health, welfare, women's rights—all paint a picture of the conditions that could lead to civil war. The UNDP annual report shows that those countries that suffer from high levels of economic distress also tend to come up short on other social welfare indicators. Poorer countries are less able to provide for the social welfare of their people, which in the data shows up as poor health, high infant mortality, and low education. The data show that three-quarters of the countries at civil war are ranked by the UNDP in the bottom half of all countries in the world on indicators of human development, and 60 percent of them are in the bottom 25 percent of the global rankings. Countries with short life expectancies, low literacy rates, high infant mortality rates, and high rates of poverty seem to have a lot of people motivated enough to take up arms against their governments. The three countries that do not report enough data for the UNDP to rank them, Côte d'Ivoire, Liberia, and Somalia, tend to be poster children for poor economic conditions, and intuition would suggest that they are also in the bottom 25 percent of all the countries in the world. These data can be found in the table at the end of the book.

Research done by the World Bank, which has a vested interest in understanding the implications of poverty, shows that under certain conditions economic growth can reduce the tendency for groups to take up arms against their governments. However, economic growth, according to this study, is simply not enough to ward off the pressures of poverty and other forces that drive individuals to join groups waging an insurgency. The World Bank report also argued rather strongly that poverty is at the core of the problem of civil wars, and also, as you might expect, civil wars create more poverty. Unrest, insurgency, and civil war are clearly not conditions conducive to economic growth, development, or political progress. A country at war, then, spirals into a vicious cycle in which poverty begets civil wars and civil wars beget more poverty.

Many of these economic stress points were evident in those countries I traveled in during times of uprising or civil war. Either the people were poor or the level of inequality in the distribution of the country's wealth was extreme and easily visible. Guatemala was desperately poor, its distribution of income one of the worst in the world. Northern Ireland wasn't poor by contemporary standards, but the Catholics got much less than the Protestants, and were keenly aware of it. In the Palestinian Territories there is no meaningful comparison to conditions in Israel, especially to those looking out from the refugee camps. In Nicaragua and Bangladesh, too, the stresses on the population were painfully obvious. From the World Bank and International Monetary Fund evidence, and my own experiences, economics invariably filters to the top. We can't know for certain what is going on in the mind of the individual, but we can draw inferences from data that converge with our intuition: poverty is the foundation upon which civil wars are built.

We cannot hope to find "the" cause, even if there were just one cause, from all these data or from intuition. It is not credible to think that a cataclysmic event like the genocide in Rwanda or Darfur happened overnight, or that the events in Sudan have one simple explanation. We can, however, understand the factors contributing to the motivation to rebel as a complex interaction of difficult economic times. Rebellion is not so much like a disease caused by a single organism, but rather like a condition brought on by a multitude of long-term habits. Poor diet, smoking, and lack of exercise can all come together to cause a heart attack. The event at a point in time is really the convergence of several factors over an extended period. Nor does a heart attack befall every unfit person, but the odds that it will happen to such a person are greater, because the conditions have been put in place for it. And, unlike a disease caused by bacteria that may be cured by targeting the bacteria, a condition such as heart failure has to be treated, once it has happened, first by repairing the damage, but finally by changing the conditions that caused it. Rebellion, likewise, does not happen overnight, nor does it happen every time the conditions are in place for it. But the likelihood for rebellion is greater in those countries where the conditions of poverty, inequity, and despair have existed for a time. The world community often attempts to repair the damage after the fact with food and medical aid in refugee camps, administering shock for heart failure, but these measures do not change the conditions that caused it in the first place, and are not a final, or even long-term, cure.

Sometimes, though a country is poor and many of its citizens are desperately poor, and inflation and economic decline are ravaging purchasing power, there will be no armed rebellion in any given year. As in 2002, there are clear indications of economic distress in the data on a number of countries that were not at war. It is easy to underestimate the inertia working against a large-scale rebellion. Because rebellion is so risky, it takes an awful lot to get the average person to take up a gun against his government. An average person who may love her country, may be nationalistic and patriotic, and may have close ties to the local community will not easily exchange the plow, the bellows, or the pen to challenge the government by force of arms. With this choice, after all, comes the risk of imprisonment, torture, and death. Nor is it that simple in practical terms to take that step.

For example, as a disgruntled citizen, I simply would not know how to join an armed opposition group, or where to begin on the road to civil war. Most people would face that same dilemma whether they are landless peasants or unemployed factory workers. But we know that when the conditions exist, someone will find these people, and the meetings, the groups, and the arms will find each other. They are also more likely to do so when the pool of people who can be motivated to join a rebel army is large.

If we look for a moment at the countries that were not doing well economically and yet were not facing insurgent movements, at least in 2002, we could conclude that economic problems, even a confluence of them, are not enough to cause a rebellion. But to draw inferences from the lack of a war in an economically challenged country in any particular year is to miss the possibility that the war might start the next year, or the next, or the one after. Only when the economic problems of a country and the public disenchantment with the policies of their government converge with the emergence of a rebel leadership will rebellion begin to look more likely. This could happen in the first year, or it could take a decade, but the causes would still be the same. Countries that are experiencing economic downturns are at a much greater risk of their citizens turning against the government.

Who fights in a rebel army is a fascinating question. The romantic image of being a rebel soldier is unrealistic when you think about the life and struggles that they face, but knowing who they are and why they fight is important. If I had to be in a rebel army I would strongly prefer leading the rebellion to being a foot soldier. One of the critical elements to orchestrating an effective rebel movement is for the people at the top of the pyramid to entice enough people to join in at the bottom. To do this they must be able to portray a better life at the end of what hopefully would be a short struggle. This requires enough people who are willing to risk most of what they have on that dim chance for change. Groups of people of similar culture, similar political orientation, or similar religion often form the backbone of armed struggles. Groups that share common traits and similar struggles can give meaning to commitment, reason to sacrifice, and provide alternatives to current conditions.

My recent foray into the intrigue of the Palestinian resistance movement gave me further insight into this process. I met Palestinians who bemoaned their economic plight but concluded that living under occupation was the best they would get, that it was pointless to fight it. Students on a college campus were painfully aware of the plight of the Palestinians as a group, of their economic difficulties, and of the inequalities between them and the Israelis. But they were—at least outwardly—less willing to admit to taking up arms to fight Israel, and they were—again at least outwardly—able to afford to go to university. All of the economic and political difficulties they faced were just not enough to get the educated middle class to take up arms. But the story in the refugee camps is different. Though they have the same history of occupation and discrimination, their expectations of the future are considerably lower. In the camps there is a hierarchy and a leadership that continues to feed the resistance in spite of Israeli efforts to stamp it out.

The role of economic distress is at the core of understanding when the individual will join up with a rebel army. But there are other influences that matter. Even highly motivated people are pushed or pulled by friends, peers, and other social pressures to either support their government or to challenge it. To understand why civil wars start we have to comprehend how this complex mix comes together in a way that encourages an individual to form or join groups, and to decide that his objectives are better served by breaking with his political leaders, and then to choose guns and bombs over ballots and petitions to do so. To understand how these individual threads weave together to form the fabric of a revolution, we must examine the warp and weft of culture and politics.

WHO FIGHTS?

7

♦ ♦ ♦

EXCLUSION AND SOLIDARITY

Rwanda 1994 was a contemporary genocide of dramatic proportions. Thousands were hacked to death with machetes while they huddled in churches seeking refuge. The world only watched as this slaughter unfolded. Debates in the UN Security Council were full of the right words, but none of the right actions. Afterwards we reflected in agony. But in spite of prior knowledge of what was to happen, there was deathly inaction before and throughout the months of carnage. People in senior policy positions claimed they did not know what to do.

When Rwanda convulsed into mass murder and terror, the distinguishing characteristic determining who killed and who died broke along lines of ethnic identification. Hutus slaughtered the Tutsis. Could a difference in ethnic identities really lead to such carnage? Could any one group of people really attempt to annihilate another simply because of a cultural or linguistic or racial dissimilarity? A genocide as systematic as this one could not have been the result of individual Hutus waking up one day and deciding to kill as many Tutsis as possible. There was a history and a legacy, and part of that legacy is tied to colonialism.

The history of Rwanda is one of tension and violence between Hutus and Tutsis, fueled by colonial policy. The Germans, and later the Belgians, created a system of discrimination between two groups of basically similar people, and then elevated the minority Tutsis over the majority Hutus. Riots and revolts became part of the Rwandan experience after the end of colonial rule. Before the genocide, Rwanda had completed the process of negotiating an end to the civil war that had ruined the country. A critical part of the agreement was a power-sharing arrangement between the Hutus and Tutsis. Although not a time of peace, this was at least a time of hope.

Political clout within Rwanda was distributed in a way that did not reflect the makeup of the population. Tutsis make up about 14 percent of the Rwandan population, Hutus 86 percent. Because of Belgian policy Tutsis occupied the political and bureaucratic hierarchy and Hutus were farmers, shopkeepers, peasants. With political power comes economic clout—the ability to distribute resources. And with political independence from the Belgians the Hutus took control and began murderous campaigns against the Tutsi, who fought back in a civil war in 1992. A peace agreement that ended the war failed, and with it went any pretense of human civility. When the Hutu took power they not only discriminated against the minority, they took out their vengeance by trying to exterminate it. The killing that ensued was so systematic that there were reports of a steady flow of bodies washing down the rivers. The exact number of people killed will never be known, but low estimates put the total at half a million, and high ones, a million. Every day, for three months, between five and ten thousand people were hacked or shot to death. Eventually Tutsis organized in their own defense and in the fighting that followed, ended up controlling the government and expelling the perpetrators of the genocide. The expelled Hutus made their way to refugee camps in the Democratic Republic of the Congo, some say under protection of the French Foreign Legion, and many would say that these encampments were the prelude to further slaughter.

What happened was the result of a collision of culture, politics, and policy. The policy was in the privileged losing some of their privilege. The politics was in the distribution of political authority, the politics was in the peace agreement, the politics was in the inability of the United Nations or any other country to stand up to the challenge of what they knew was coming.

Rwanda is used as an example of "ethnic war." Focusing on ethnicity in this way puts the emphasis in the wrong place. Ethnicity mattered, of course, but only to the extent that it identified who was killed and who did the killing. It is not the cause, nor does it provide the explanation for why this genocide happened. And the reasons are well removed from questions of hatred.

From Beslan, Russia, came news coverage of a massacre. One hundred and eighty-six of the dead were children, placed in rows outside their school where it had taken place. We see Iraqi bodies on the news every day, brought out of smoldering remains of cars, or skeletons of marketplaces, and laid out in the street over blood and oil. These images, be they from Kashmir, Chechnya, Bosnia, or Darfur, are overlaid with confident, sober voices of news anchors and embedded reporters emphasizing, by constant repetition, "ethnic hatred," "ethnic cleansing," "religious violence," "sectarian fighting." Such labels are part of the language used to characterize civil wars. We have internalized these characterizations, and accept that these wars derive from mutual and historical hatred between two groups of people. The causes of the conflicts, the ideology, the demands of the people fighting in them, are condensed into these epithets that obscure the history and belie the facts on the ground. Most tragically, the potential for answers that lie within the causes is lost. The solutions to any problem, whether psychological, environmental, or social, is found in the causes. In misconstruing the causes of civil wars, the possibility for success in preventing or stopping these wars is diminished, at best. At worst, misunderstanding at such a basic level only exacerbates the issues.

It is not the case, however, that identity—whether based in race, religion, ethnicity, or ideology—plays no part in the process of civil wars. Quite the opposite. Most of the fighters in a particular rebel army are of the same color, or revere the same prophet, or at least speak the same dialect. They don't end up on the same side by random chance. Their identity is clearly important. They live together, they pray together, they suffer together, and they fight together. The question really is, what part does their color, their prophet, or their dialect play in the war they fight? Are any of these the reason they find themselves carrying a Kalashnikov or planting landmines?

My experience and the evidence that I can bring to bear suggest that these wars are not about ethnicity, whatever the popular notion. These are not "ethnic wars" in the sense that people fight because of their or their enemy's ethnicity. These are political wars that break along ethnic lines. That distinction is important.

Take, for example, the long-running Irish Troubles. I couldn't tell, just by looking at two people, which one of them was a Catholic and which a Protestant in Northern Ireland or, for that matter, Germany or France. Not only would they look and sound the same, I would guess, they pray to the same god. But certainly in Northern Ireland they found a way to distribute the resources of the province in a manner that found many more Catholics fighting British control than Protestants. The Irish Republican Army is made up almost entirely of Catholics. But Catholicism and Protestantism in opposition does not seem a credible explanation for thirty years of "the struggles." That conflict has long roots in discrimination, oppression, and the legacy of an imperial past.

The conflict in Darfur, Sudan, is another study in how civil wars are presented to us as ethnic wars. The people in Darfur being exploited, raped, killed, and forced to flee to refugee camps are nearly all Blacks. The rebel army trying to defend this group of people and their region face a determined Sudanese government and the Janjaweed, a militia the government supports. The Janjaweed is made up of Arabic Sudanese who also live in this region of Sudan. To the untrained eye this conflict looks like a struggle between nomadic Arabic peoples and pastoral Black people, driven by their ethnic differences. The media refers to it, almost always, as an ethnic war, reinforcing the impression that one group is bent on the destruction of the other for no reason other than their otherness. It would be more productive, in the interest of finding a solution, to think about this civil war in terms of resources and competition for control over decreasing amounts of farmland and water. The region is being lost to an encroaching desert, and as a result, there is less arable land to farm and less water to irrigate crops. Rights to ownership and access to land and water are a form of distribution of the country's resources that will be determined by the government, the gun, or both. According to a report by the British

House of Commons, the pastoral people are worried they will be shut out of access to water and land altogether—worried enough to fight. The Janjaweed and the government are pushing them off the land and so pushing them increasingly closer to the margins of existence. They certainly don't have the political clout to make sure they have continued access to the resources necessary to maintain their way of life. They lose out as the shared resources shrink. One group, in this case the Blacks, being excluded and shut out of political power, creates a form of structural poverty.

Focusing primarily on the ethnic characteristics of the participants in this war makes it sound as if Blacks and Arabs pose a threat to the culture and stability of the other. Since conventional "wisdom" has conditioned us to look for a clash of cultures, we read and accept this situation as two groups that can't get along because of their racial or ethnic differences. In fact conventional wisdom would have us believe these two groups of people despise each other so much that they will incur all the risks associated with war because of their aversion to each other. To believe that differences in identity are enough to make a group of people want to kill each other would be to assume that identities—based on race, religion, or language—are so strong in themselves as to overcome normal social behavior. It would be to ignore all the examples of countries and peoples living with tolerance and relative harmony amidst diversity. It is hard to imagine a farmer risking his job, his family, and his life by joining a rebel army just to wipe out a particular ethnic group. He might not like people of that ethnic group, he might not want to do business with them, and he might not choose to marry one of them. But the average person is not likely to risk his life to get rid of them. In effect, it would be unlikely that a rebel leader could convince enough members of his ethnic group to take that risk. There would be some who would join up, but not enough for an army. Unless that identity is significant in some way other than just as a cultural difference. Unless that identity has been used to oppress the group politically, economically, or both, and has threatened their way of life or existence.

As with most other aspects of trying to understand civil wars, there are statistical data that can determine the influence of ethnic or cultural patterns on civil war. The strongest part of the evidence suggests that if there is a dominant group concentrated within one country, chances of civil war are higher. Concentration is the numerical dominance of one cultural group over others. This type of dominance often results in political exclusion and economic discrimination. For example, in Turkey ethnic Turks make up about 80 percent of the population, ethnic Kurds the other 20 percent. It shouldn't surprise you that the Turks dominate the political process and discriminate against the Kurds. This points right back to the idea that politics is at the heart of civil wars, and that the political system is doing a poor job of taking all of its citizens into account. Catholics in Northern Ireland, Palestinians in the Occupied Territories, Kurds in Turkey and in Iraq before the latest war, the Karen in Burma, and Blacks in Darfur are all examples of groups politically and economically dominated within their countries.

In 1981 I joined the Peace Corps. In the months between college and my departure I took a trip with my duffel bag and guitar hitchhiking south to Florida and back up to Washington, D.C. At the time my friends would have described me as politically progressive. I was progressive in terms of whom to vote for, what social policies were best for our society, and the role of the military in domestic and foreign policy. I had signed up with a U.S. government agency, so I was far from being an anarchist or a revolutionary. One of my rides from Florida was in the back of a pickup truck with a young couple on their way to College Park, Maryland. They invited me to their friend's house, which gave me a place to stay, some camaraderie, and an unexpected education. We talked politics well into the night; the discussions were fascinating. This group of people was well informed, well read, and angry. Their talk soon turned to the violent overthrow of the U.S. government, and plans to blow up government buildings. My notion of what it meant to be politically progressive took a sharp turn. Throughout the night—and it was a long one—we talked about engaging in the political process rather than trying to subvert it. They would have none of it. The system, to them, was wrong and had to be brought down.

What these people had in common was their near-total disregard for the legitimacy of the U.S. government. There was no common religious or ethnic identity among them. The struggles in the United States during the 1960s and 1970s will attest to the fact that not all groups are antigovernment. The link among those who wanted to overthrow the government then was not race, religion, or ethnicity.

Although my new friends invited me to stay as long as I wanted, I left in the morning. I did not wish to get swept up in the violence, nor did I want to be there if the FBI broke the door down. Simply put, I was afraid to stay in that house because the consequences of mere association with their cause were more than I could contemplate. Being even on the fringe of a revolutionary movement was scary. I left with a new understanding of what it meant to want to change policies, to overthrow a government, and to be a revolutionary. These were the future elite corps of a rebel movement. The next night I stayed in a homeless shelter. That was an entirely different lesson.

If it is often easy to identify distinct groups within a society, and if the political system systematically discriminates against one group to the benefit of another, then the foundation is laid, at least, for one group to feel disaffected by the system that keeps them down.

In the United States there is a history of trying to convince white people that blacks are inferior, even when there is no evidence to support this. I grew up in a community that tried desperately to make us all believe it. If we did, bussing would be rejected, blacks wouldn't move into "our" neighborhoods, we would eliminate competition for jobs and other social goods. Cultural hatred can be created in this way, and if a community works at it long enough, the hatred itself begins to look like the cause.

When I went to Guatemala I encountered an amazing group of people, particularly in the rural areas. Their dress was so colorful; they sold little handicrafts; they looked so desperately poor; and to me at least, they seemed incredibly meek and humble. Yet these indigenous people, Mayans, were subjected to inordinate abuse by the Guatemalan government. These were also the people who in overwhelming numbers were represented in the rebel organization. The Mayan ancestry goes back to the great civilizations of Central America, and they retain their positions as farmers and peasants in the rural economy. They also have physical characteristics that make them distinguishable from the mixed-race people who reside in the cities and who run the country. The Mayans of Guatemala have two characteristics that help lump them into a common group: ethnic lineage and social standing. Both these traits contributed to the ease with which policies of the government and the economic system could discriminate against them.

I learned about being on the other side on a twenty-four-hour journey in a bus from the remote Tikal region of Guatemala to the capital city. I took this trip with a lawyer I had made friends with in Tikal. Most of the people on the bus were the poor indigenous people, those from whom the government felt the greatest threat. That in itself always struck me as odd. These people seemed to me nonthreatening, in fact weak and meek, compared to the soldiers and the people who occupied the cities. On that bus ride we were stopped by the military six times in twenty-four hours. Each time the soldiers would take everyone off and have the men spread-eagled against the side of the bus. One by one they put a rifle in our backs, asked for documents, and gave us a thorough frisking. Other soldiers searched the bus. After the third time I decided I'd had enough of this frightening and humiliating experience. The next time we were stopped I walked away from the bus, refusing to be searched or intimidated. Three soldiers approached with their rifles pointed at me. I submitted immediately. When we got back on the bus my friend warned me not to be so foolish again. His warning was not necessary. At the next military patrol I lined up with everyone else along the side of the bus.

The experience gave me the gift of knowing the humiliation of not being in control, the anger of being powerless to change my situation, frustration from the inability to express what I felt, cold fear of what might happen to me if I did. I wondered how it might be for my fellow travelers. This was their life, not just the single journey it was for me. The experience showed me how the policies of the government can contribute to the attitudes and perceptions of their subjects.

There is a critical process that turns motivation into action. The people on that bus may be miserably poor and utterly unhappy with their lot in life. They might even be willing to endure hardship because those were the cards they were dealt. But to suffer humiliation, indignity, and fear because of being identified with a specific group can pull even the most reluctant person into the rebel corner. Every day this can describe the Palestinian at an Israeli checkpoint, the Muslim in a U.S. airport, the black person in a white neighborhood. Group identification works to push and pull on motivations that begin as economic grievances. Civil wars are group events, and to fully understand how they start and stop we have to develop a picture of how various elements of group identity make risky choices palatable.

If the economy is doing very well, discrimination might not be enough to get an individual to risk revolt. But in difficult economic times, such as in Darfur, the choice may be made considerably easier by the fact that some groups get singled out by the policies of the government, to the point of endangering their existence. Group identity, that is, can form the backbone of the policies of discrimination. If the poverty or dire economic conditions affect one group disproportionately, then this group of people has a common link through their grievances and a common source for their motivation.

Identity, then, is an important factor in civil wars only *after* it has become politicized, by being made a criterion for exclusion. Identity is only identity until it is used to discriminate against, to exclude, a particular group. People are black or white, pastoral or nomadic, Hindu, Muslim, or Jewish. Once the identity of a group is used against them, it takes on political meaning, and then it is deployed by those who would mobilize the group to rise up against the dominant other in the struggle for political access, for justice. Identity, then, becomes the tool for mobilization, and is further politicized. The very discrimination that caused a group's identity to be something other than just group identity—be that a common language or a common religion—now becomes a bond that is rooted in grievance and suffering. This is the part of a group's identity that will be emphasized, recalled, used by rebel leaders to incite anger, to call to the cause. They will exploit it to fan the flames of hatred, communalism, and fanaticism in order to fill the ranks of the rebel army. In the academic world this is called ethnic entrepreneurship.

Throughout the 1990s, Charles Taylor fomented a civil war in Liberia that pitted ethnic groups against each other. He recruited soldiers from the ranks of those who were dispossessed and oppressed by Samuel Doe, the man he wanted to overthrow. He fed these new recruits on drugs and hatred and turned them loose to plunder and rape their fellow citizens. These rebels were responsible for brutal atrocities on civilians—mutilations, kidnappings, deaths in the tens of thousands. Both Taylor and the international community portrayed the conflict as tribal wars rooted in ethnic hatred. But this conflict was more the result of corruption and discrimination stemming from poverty and the struggle over access to the country's wealth. Taylor played up ethnic divisions to mobilize those who did the raping and killing. Charles Taylor went on trial for war crimes and crimes against humanity, including the systematic rape of women and the use of children as soldiers. The world community ignored the events in Liberia for many reasons, but none good enough to have abandoned the people to that war and the horrors that were visited upon them.

People share languages, mythologies that constitute their history, that link them as a group. These are passed on through generations, strengthening the bonds of the group, cementing the identity of the individual as belonging to that group. You might think that any strong cultural links between Irish Americans and Ireland have long ago fragmented into the potpourri of the United States. But memories of a potato famine and treatment received at the hands of the British are kept alive. This was, after all, what turned many of our forebears into immigrants. There are stories of ill treatment in the cities across the United States only a generation or two ago, of the path out of the ghetto through police and fire departments, and the perception of this group from the outside, the reputation of drinking and fighting too much, of breeding too fast. Even though the German, Italian, and Polish communities have similar stories, they each have their own exclusive membership. This unique narrative gives information to those on the inside about who helps them and who hurts them, who their persecutors are, and where to look for a way out.

Every group has their victories and defeats, their horrors and the heroes who stood up to inequities. They are chronicled, remembered.

October 29, 1956, Kafr Qassem: forty-seven Palestinian Arab men, women, and children returning home from the fields were shot and killed by Israeli troops for violating a curfew placed on their village that they had no knowledge of. Bloody Sunday, January 30, 1972, Derry: British soldiers killed thirteen unarmed men at a civil rights march. April 13, 1919, Amritsar, India: the British killed hundreds of peaceful protesters, known generally as the Jalianwalla massacre. April 9, 1948, the village of Deir Yassin: the massacre of two hundred and fifty Palestinians by Israeli militia under the command of Menachem Begin, said to be a major cause of the Nakba, the exodus of some half million Palestinians from their homeland. These events are kept alive through generations; they are knots tying groups together with the memory of shared trauma, of atrocities never to be forgotten. No Jew in the world will ever forget their history of oppression. Support for the creation of the state of Israel depended in large part on the guilt for the Holocaust and the memory of persecution that goes back beyond biblical times. In American mythology every kid learns to remember the Alamo. Now everyone will learn of 9/11.

In thinking about the conflict in Israel and the Occupied Territories it is nearly impossible to strip away Palestinian and Israeli histories from the issues that compel them to kill each other. Palestinian college students I met spoke of the necessity of the struggle rooted in history, a narrative that portrays participation in a violent struggle as honorable. I shared an airport taxi with a small group of Israeli Jews. They defined their struggle by reference to Masada, site of a heroic last stand by a group of embattled Jews in the year A.D. 66. The documentary *A Death in Gaza* follows the transformation of Palestinian children. At a young age there is already development of signals and cues that keep Palestinians growing up to be martyrs, just as there are stories and cues that keep the Israelis fighting for their political and social survival.

Group affiliation influences an individual's choice to either join the rebels, support the government, or do nothing. Being poor and alone is not the stuff of civil wars. And if the civil war expands, that option of sitting it out becomes increasingly difficult. There are few other choices available.

In spite of all the hardship and abuse at the hands of a government that is sworn to protect and defend its citizens, it does not make a lot of sense to support the rebels, at least if you think things through logically. At some level of consciousness every potential rebel recruit must consider what he stands to gain and lose by joining the insurgency. Recognizing the risks is quite easy. Even if a person waxes poetic about being a rebel soldier, he would still have to consider that, after he has risked life and limb, the most important spoils of victory go to everyone equally, to the whole country. Even those who don't participate, the free riders, get the new form of government or the new distribution of resources. One person can sit on the sidelines and hide from the struggle, while another risks liberty, family, and life, and in the end they both share equally in the bounty. So why would anyone choose the life of the rebel soldier? Logically, nobody would join up with the rebel leadership, and eventually an armed struggle would falter. This is in fact what happens most of the time. Without being quite so explicit in *The Grapes of Wrath*, Steinbeck describes the "Okies" facing this very problem when they reached California. They were neglected, abused, impoverished, exploited, and they all knew it. But as a group they were unable to overcome the difficulties associated with group action. In the end they all suffered because everyone was hungry and not enough people would pay the individual price required for a collective outcome.

A political outcome in which everybody shares equally is called a collective good. Collective goods are everywhere in our lives. Clean water and air and military security are collective goods. If an individual or organization spends time, effort, and money to bring down the level of pollution, everyone benefits from the resulting clean air. No one person can be excluded from breathing. Armed insurgencies function this same way. If there is a sweeping change as a result of a civil war, everybody will benefit from the change, including those who did not take the risks that were necessary to achieve that change.

No one person, however disillusioned or angered by discrimination, can wage war by himself. To get to a civil war there must be some serious and effective effort to mobilize the masses against the government. Mobilization is key. Efforts to mobilize a rebel army must overcome the tendency of people to let others take the risks and hope that the outcome plays out in their favor.

So what can be done about this dilemma of collective action? I think back to Quilali, Nicaragua. I had a feeling about the town, about the absence of all the men, a sense that it was a collective decision. If not consciously collective, several individual decisions that, when seen together, looked as if the town had chosen a common action. I knew I was in a war zone, but it was still not intuitive to think that so many of the men had gone to fight. If we think in terms of a single individual who has grievances against his government, and examine what it would take to get him to go out into the jungle, it begins to look unlikely that he would. First, he would have to leave friends and family after at least attempting to convince them he was doing the right thing. One of them would certainly ask him about his thoughts on winning the war, on getting caught and suffering punishment, on his expectations for a better life after the war was over. And in this discussion somebody would certainly point out to him that he could not win the war by himself, that he would need others to join in the struggle.

Given that the risks are high and the outcome precarious, why would even one individual, let alone so many of the young men in that small town in northern Nicaragua, make that choice? At the time, the United States was funding a rebel army to challenge the Sandinista government for control. The United States was paying the local people to fight on their side of the war. To that individual recruit, the Contra army was paying a selective benefit, some payment in cash or kind that made it worth all the risks and in fact changed some of the calculations about what he might consider a rational course of action. Even if the people of Quilali, Nicaragua, were not terribly disgruntled with the Sandinista government—and there is evidence they were—and if the United States was paying them considerably more than they could earn farming, then any one individual might find it appealing to go fight with a rebel army.

This is not that different from what governments do to recruit soldiers. In the United States, a considerable proportion of the enlisted forces come from lower socioeconomic communities. Recruits are paid for their services—often not much more than they would earn at McDonald's. They also incur the risks of having to go fight. The cause they fight for might not be one they are most concerned about, but many of them do so because the salary of a marine is better than other options available to them. They can be trained to fight for love of country, but selective benefits, such as college tuition, signing bonuses, and a living wage, are often necessary to get them to sign up for the fight. In Quilali the payment of selective benefits might have been enough to sway the loyalties of much of the town. By itself, payment from the United States was not enough to get the town to support the rebels, but combined with existing grievances the money helped overcome the incentives not to fight, especially in a poor town in a poor country.

Group affinity, shared mythology, and a common history also provide some of the selective incentives for mobilization. These come with membership in a specific ethnic group. To put it differently, not everybody signs up to fight with the highest bidder. Political scientist Jeremy Weinstein at Stanford University provides an interesting way to think about the difference between those who fight because of commitment to a group and those who fight for money.

R esearch tells us that the larger the group, the more difficult it is to achieve an efficient level of collective action. This is because the larger the number of people, the less likely it is that each individual can make a significant difference in whether or not the group accomplishes its goal. An individual can make a rational decision to not participate, and still expect that enough others will. But if every individual takes this route, there is little hope of achieving the goal. Think about it from the perspective of a rebel army of ten thousand soldiers. If a single soldier defects from the group, she will not have a perceptible impact on the ability to win the war. It makes sense, therefore, for an individual to avoid participation in the insurgency. And if the insurgency is successful she still shares in the rewards. But if every potential rebel soldier makes this calculation, there will be no rebel army. To be effective something has to work against this incentive to not participate.

In small groups the dynamics are a bit different, and it is in fact easier to generate participation. Because any one defection from the group is easy to identify, and because any one defection will perceptibly decrease the chances of victory, there will be more of an incentive to participate with the group. Small groups turn out to be better organized than large ones, but small armies cannot be very effective against what are almost always much larger government forces. Since rebels need a big army rather than a small one, the leaders must have some way to overcome the problems of generating collective action. Any local peace activist or an organizer around the abortion rights debate will confirm that many more people support their cause than show up at rallies. It is impossible to get all the supporters to come out on the streets. This is the collective action problem at work. The larger the pool of unhappy people, the easier it is for any one individual to duck out of taking risks. Push this to the extreme, and everybody ducks and there is no serious effort to confront the government. So when we do see a civil war we know that there are some strong group dynamics at work.

If it is so difficult to overcome the collective incentives to avoid action, how is it that rebel leaders are able to recruit soldiers? The answers lie partially in the nature of group cohesion and common identities among people. Irish Catholics versus Irish Protestants, Sinhalese Sri Lankans versus Tamil Sri Lankans, Jews versus Muslims, or as in our most destructive contemporary conflict, Blacks versus Arabs in Darfur, Sudan. It is this group cohesiveness that mistakenly gets journalists, policy makers, and even academics thinking about ethnic wars rather than the less loaded concept of civil wars or insurrections. When we mistake the role of group identity for the cause, we miss the motivations behind civil wars.

When the system is working well and there is little to complain about, history becomes part of cultural folklore, like Irish American lore today. But if the group is threatened by policies that work against its members, collective pain may translate into collective indignation, and ultimately into collective demands on the government. Without the shared history, culture, myths, and heroes there will be fewer members willing to incur the risk of rebellion alongside those with whom they share only the discrimination. To scholars who study civil wars the role of culture in mobilizing people is thought of in terms of the mobilization of resources. You can't have a civil war unless you mobilize your resources to support the cause.

If the discrimination is targeted at members of a specific group— or at least is perceived to be so—then grievances will be vented within the group. So what do groups have in common that will facilitate this? Members might attend the same church, the same social clubs, the same schools. Laborers work in the same factories or fields, and live in the same communities. In short, they have many ways to make contacts, to air their grievances, to shape their demands. Members of a group also have a history, often of a struggle where the leaders of the struggle have become the local heroes or legends. Those who stood up to the inequities of the system also stand up as role models within the group. The struggles, the history, and the fight live on within the group, even if only simmering below the surface. The shared stories, cues, and language of struggle provide a way for individual members to become tied to the past, tied to the heroes, and tied to the struggle. Outsiders can easily be excluded, and committed rebel soldiers more easily recruited. In the complex brew that generates civil wars ethnicity is an identifier for discrimination and a tool for mobilization. But it is not a *cause de guerre*.

There is a sequence of events in an individual's life that can go from a grinding struggle to the decision to join a rebel army. The political process and the response of the government to the demands of the opposition drive much of this sequence. The story is not complete without an understanding of how this response by the government can make or break the peace.

8

♦ ♦ ♦

BLOODY FAVORITISM

Civil war, although inefficient, costly, and violent, is a form of political participation. Armed insurrection is an attempt, maybe a last resort, for those shut out of the political process to get what they believe to be their due. Civil wars are political events defined by political processes.

Belfast in the winter of 1981 looked and felt like a war zone. British soldiers with semiautomatic rifles were a threatening and oppressive presence. Young men, armed and masked, looked down from murals that covered entire building walls. Some had names and dates—those who had given their lives to the struggle. I was to see this iconography again, in a different time and place—the winter of 2006 in the towns and refugee camps of Palestine. They command awe and inspiration from their people, these martyrs. They promise a better life to those who join the fight, either here or in heaven.

Emotions were high in Northern Ireland, the schism visible in every aspect of life. Even as an American hitchhiking through the country, I was asked at every inn whether I was Catholic or Protestant. With a name like mine, I couldn't hide it anyway. My sympathies were assumed to be on the Catholic side of the conflict. In Enniskillen, near the southern border, in a sleazy bar I met a man who found my transience and foreignness nonthreatening enough to make me his confessor for the night. He bought me a Guinness, and after drinking an alarming quantity himself, told me about the recent murder of a police officer. The officer had been walking through a field with his daughter when the IRA shot him down. My companion claimed to have been on the planning team. When I expressed doubts about the merit of shooting a civilian, he stopped me short. The dead man was not just an innocent civilian. He was part of the occupying force; he upheld the rule of the British. I arranged to meet my drinking partner again the next day, but he didn't show. Either too much drink or too much talk kept him away, but I did confirm the basic facts of his story. Whether he told me the truth about his involvement or just recounted a story from the morning paper, his passion and determination revealed the strength of his feelings about right and wrong in his narrow world. I was left with a heightened sense of how committed these people were to forcing change. Catholics desired unification with the "free state"—what most of us think of as Ireland. Protestants supported an official affiliation with Britain. The Protestants got more from their affiliation than the Catholics, who certainly got less than they would as part of greater Ireland.

Poverty is an economic issue, but it is politics that often determines who will be landless and who has access to clean water and medical care. Politics determines who is poor and who has plenty. Economic issues have roots in the political world. These domains may seem so intertwined as to be virtually inseparable. But to understand how politics shapes the economy it is worthwhile to think of them as two separate issues.

It is easy for those who hold political power to favor their own when it comes to the distribution of resources, and to do so at the expense of others. Protestants in Northern Ireland, Jews in Israel, Arabs in Sudan—all groups in power—distribute the wealth of their country to their own people. Catholics, Palestinians, Blacks in Sudan—ones left out of a fair share—are impoverished if the resources are meager or dwindling, and are not unaware that it takes political access to control the resources of the country. These groups fight to gain that access. When the disenfranchised see the policies of the government working to keep them out of the economic wealth of their country, it becomes all the more urgent that they gain political power, and with it the ability to redistribute resources to their advantage and ameliorate their situation.

Clear evidence of the role of politics in resource distribution within a country is difficult to come by. It is nearly impossible, for example, to find data on the ethnic or religious makeup of those who rule a country, or how they pass out wealth. What we can do is describe how politics interacts with cultural identity to cause a skewed distribution and create circumstances that lead to civil war.

Suppose there is a country with two main ethnic groups, making up 53 percent and 47 percent of the population respectively. Though not always the case, it is often the majority, even a slim one, that controls most of the positions of power. Saddam Hussein, though from the Sunni minority, made very sure that the majority Shia population got much less than their due. He managed to pull this off by the sheer brutality of his rule. Given a fair distribution, the minority group in our hypothetical example could reasonably expect to receive 47 percent of the national resources. The way politics plays out, though, does not guarantee this. In the political world, as in a corporation, those with 53 percent of the voting stock have complete control over decision making. In the political world this can be destabilizing. Imagine the attitude of that 47 percent minority when they get considerably less than 47 percent of the goods. Consider the implications if the distribution were not just skewed, but grossly so, if those who held power gave the minority group only 30 percent of the goods and took that extra 17 percent for themselves.

Regardless of the type of political system a country has, a particular group of people determines the tax rate, the official language, what goods the government will subsidize, where schools and hospitals are located and who gets access to them, whether unions have the right to organize, the punishments for violating even the most basic laws. There are myriad ways that governments pass out the financial and social privileges they control, and politics determines which individuals have access to how much of those resources. The politics behind these processes is not always transparent, but it is clear that power determines the results, and whom they affect.

The poor need subsidies for transportation, cooking oils, fuels. The politically connected must be willing to provide them. For those living at the margins a cooking oil subsidy could make the difference between cooking and not. Tax breaks, road building, and infrastructure improvement are some of the ways resources are passed on to the wealthy at the expense of the poor. Although it is argued that corporate or business subsidies create jobs, it is usually not much help to those facing real economic hardship. Argentina found out in 2001 this is not always an effective strategy. The government has a fixed pot of money to distribute, and there is competition over who gets how much. Those who have political influence generally get their way, and those who do not must make do. This can be the politics of poverty and a pathway to rebellion.

Political power is instrumental in resource distribution, regardless of the type of government—democracy, monarchy, or authoritarian state. Resources are anything that the government can give out: tax relief, subsidies, roads, post offices, hospitals, military contracts, housing, education. Access to schooling, for example, will give immediate insight into how a government indirectly distributes wealth. If the school system is public, then access to an education is held as a public trust. In most countries, however, not everyone gets equal access. Blacks in the United States, particularly in the South, in the 1940s and 1950s did not get a share of the government's education monies commensurate with their percentage of the population. Blacks could not get an education equal to whites, and over time the income of the white population grew disproportionately to that of the black population. These decisions made in the twentieth century were politically driven choices to distribute resources in a distinct pattern that discriminated overwhelmingly against one racial group and privileged another.

Not only did the black community get less than a fair share of resources, they were also excluded from power. Four black members have been elected to the U.S. Senate in its history, and between 1930 and 1970, eight to the House of Representatives. Clearly the black population did not have access to the mechanisms that distributed the wealth of the U.S. government. History suggests that they are all too aware of being shortchanged by the very system that should protect and defend them.

The point here is not that the distribution of resources and political power in the United States is skewed, but rather that one of the primary roles of government in all countries is to distribute resources, and that most do so in reasonably predictable ways: minority groups get less than their share. It is easy to see this in the history of the United States, but it was also evident in South Africa under Apartheid, in Guatemala and El Salvador between elite coffee growers and indigenous peoples, in Northern Ireland between Protestants and Catholics, in the Middle East between Israelis and Palestinians, and in Darfur between the Black tribal peoples and the Arabs who run the country. These are choices political leaders make. They could make different ones. The type of government doesn't change the basic fact that politics determines the distribution of resources. It is this way in the United States and South Africa and Israel.

It is difficult to think about economic demands outside of the political environment that spawned those demands. Politics can create economic winners and losers, and economic losers can, and do, create political havoc for the government.

Israel fights a persistent and dedicated insurgency waged by the Palestinians, which in the years from 2000 to 2007 has claimed more than 4,000 lives. According to the Israeli International Policy Institute for Counter-Terrorism, of those 4,000 killed, 1,700 have been noncombatants, with almost equal numbers of noncombatants killed on each side. India contends with several regional insurgencies, the most visible being Kashmir. Great Britain fought an insurgency in its Northern Ireland province for nearly thirty years. What these countries have in common, apart from long-running insurgencies, is that they are democracies. Israel—always championed as the only democracy in the Middle East. India—the world's largest. Great Britain—one of the oldest. Turkey, the Philippines, Russia—all democracies—faced challenges from within their populations. Political pundits tell us that democracy is all we need to prevent civil wars and reduce terrorism, that there are pacifying effects of democracy. But the easy explanation that democratic government is the panacea that will solve the entire problem of civil war does not stand up to even the most cursory examination. It matters less the form of government that they live under than the politics that determines who gets what and how much of it.

If access to political power is access to resources, then those who are disenfranchised have two basic choices: endure their hardship or use the forms of political expression available to them to expose their grievances. Living in a democratic country makes the latter choice easier, but it doesn't eliminate the harsh realities that many minority groups face. Regardless of whether they are made formally in a legislative environment or through political organizing and opposition rallies, political demands are always seen as just that—demands. And political demands require political responses.

Ways to achieve immediate relief are limited for people living under economic and social policies that make daily life difficult. One approach is to organize a demonstration that will bring like-minded people out into the streets and demand attention to their issues. This option is legal even in some nondemocratic countries. The intention might not be to overthrow the government, but only to attempt to change policies that create economic adversity. But such activities run the risk of government crackdown. The organizers might hope for a different response, but the history of their country, their struggle, or a particular political movement tells them to expect the worst. If many of the potential supporters are of the same religion or ethnic origin, there is a common thread of shared history, maybe one of repression or abuse, of resistance or exclusion from political power and economic fortunes of the country. This thread is woven into the rhetoric that organizers use to convince sympathizers to take up the fight.

Most political opposition starts at a basic level. A meeting of a small central committee. A plan to engage others. A list of demands. When political organizing begins, local authorities usually have an idea of what is being planned. Participation in demonstrations presents the biggest hurdle because the collective action problem works against the organizers. People are afraid most of all of being arrested and harmed physically by authorities. This fear is precisely what authorities want.

To overcome this problem the central committee has to create a core group that would be at the front of the march, willing to shelter other participants from government response, if it is violent. Martin Luther King in U.S. civil rights marches and Mahatma Gandhi in India's independence movement were right up front getting beaten and arrested.

If the government responds to these initial demonstrations by showing a willingness to discuss demands and possible solutions, there would be positive progress. Discussions and concessions would considerably lessen chances of an armed insurgency. There would be no point in incurring the risks involved in attempting to overthrow the government when progress is made through negotiation. But when a government responds with violence, the process moves in a different direction. It is still part of a political process, but the path to change is much different. Violent government response to political demands is an early step toward civil war.

In the ensuing violence of the demonstration most people scatter and return home. The leadership, those at the front of the march, would be arrested, jailed, and possibly beaten. The government's objective is to make future political demonstrations less likely by instilling fear in the organizers and their supporters. Eventually the leaders get out of jail, perhaps hardened by the experience. This small group suffers in the process, losing jobs, or facing increasing scrutiny by the government or avoidance from members of the community who may fear to associate with them. Fidel Castro was arrested, imprisoned, released, and went on to lead a revolution. His short time in prison served him well.

If the leadership is cowed and blends back into the community, the government wins, and political demands are muted for the short term. The issues will simmer until another intrepid group takes up the challenge. But if that core group continues to organize and press the government for change, the seeds of insurgency are sown. With each demonstration government abuse gets a little more extreme, and demonstrators begin to adopt strategies in which tear gas and batons are answered by bottles, bricks, and Molotov cocktails. What could have been a political exercise in cooperation and accommodation begins to spiral into violence. This is the tragedy of how governments can generate the dynamics that lead to civil wars. Nonviolent avenues to political change begin to close as violence begets violence. Either side could still retreat, but it gets harder for the leaders of the opposition to give in. By this stage they may be underground and hunted by authorities, if not for sedition, then for other violent crimes associated with the protests.

If dissidents continue to push the government, and all peaceful avenues are continually closed, opposition leaders are compelled to organize an armed movement. They face the choice of either mobilizing a rebel army or giving up—letting fear of abuse curtail their efforts. Living another year under the current conditions might seem desirable when compared with ten years chained in a jail cell, if they are lucky. In most instances backing down is what happens. The costs of rebellion are too high and the level of support within the community too low this early in the process. Even when economic and political conditions point to the possibility of an armed rebellion, it doesn't always materialize because of the difficulty of mobilizing supporters in the face of overwhelming government power. Organizing an opposition group starts small; in the beginning, rebel groups are considerably weaker than the government. The odds are good at this stage that the government will win, and all parties know this.

In the mid-1960s in the United States, the Black Panther Party began to organize for change, or what they called liberation. Their goals were working-class emancipation and economic justice for the poor and minorities. Mass arrests of the organizers of a march on the California State Capitol led to a call to take up arms. Some of the names—Huey Newton, Bobby Seale, and David Hilliard—remain familiar. By 1968 the FBI began a systematic crackdown on groups thought to be joining the armed movement, including the Peace and Freedom Party, the Brown Berets, Students for a Democratic Society (SDS), and the Student Non-Violent Coordinating Committee (SNCC), among others. Under intense pressure from the U.S. government—violent and otherwise—the party structure fell apart by the early 1980s. The Black Panthers, and the movement they represented, never generated enough popular support to pose a credible challenge to the government. But that is not true in many other countries that face committed challenges from groups who are willing to take their struggle into the arena of violence. These relatively recent events in the U.S. political system illustrate that such political processes happen everywhere, and that they do not always take the full route to armed insurrection.

Anyone who resorts to violence for political change knows that sedition, from the government's perspective and by the law of the land, is about the worst crime they can commit. A rebel group in the mountains needs material support from local communities, and needs to avoid capture. They must overcome problems of recruitment. They must get the attention of the government and of potential rebel recruits. The insurgency would start slowly, by blowing up a bridge or a police station, some action that would put them on record as a group to contend with. At this point an individual rebel's life is virtually irreversible in the short term.

The political process, though, does not end at this stage. It is the political process that creates the distribution of resources that leads one group to make demands. It is the political process that determines whether those demands receive a violent response or are permitted to play out through formal and legal routes. And when conditions are right for resolution, it is a political process that drives negotiations to end a war.

Solutions to the Israeli-Palestinian conflict have been on the table in various forms for a generation, and the agreement that ended the Irish Troubles was possible twenty years before it happened. Politics, expectations, and attitudes have to be overcome before resolution. To ask why things ever come this far is to ask why there is not sufficient attention paid to the motivations and incentives of those who would consider armed rebellion. But it also requires thinking about why political leaders find it so difficult to make concessions to groups who do not share in political power or access. When it comes to political challenges to the distribution of wealth and power, repression appears to be the route with the least political resistance, even in democratic countries. It is easier than making concessions, but only in the short term.

Repression is terror. If sufficiently terrorized, more people will withhold support for the opposition and side with the government instead. At least, this is the theory. Both government and rebel leaders vie for the support of the people, and both do this by offering promises and using terror tactics. Promises of land reform, greater subsidies, and religious or cultural tolerance, are some of the possible enticements. The rebels can make promises conditional on victory. The government has the power to implement them immediately, giving them the upper hand. What people hope to achieve through rebellion may be had at greatly reduced cost by supporting a reform movement within the government. These concessions could be offered at the outset, but the government may think they do not have to. When concessions are on the table, rebels find themselves having to compete for the loyalties of the very people they are trying to mobilize.

The evidence suggests that governments tend to respond with repression rather than concessions, at least until it is too late. Often the repression is indiscriminate, targeting rebels, rebel supporters, and even uninvolved citizens. Indiscriminate violence by a military or a paramilitary force is very difficult to endure, and by this stage cooperation with the government might become impossible until a war has been fought. Rebels might conclude that they are better off harming those who might turn them in. The Contra in Nicaragua, for instance, were just as effective at terrorizing the local population who helped government troops as they were at fighting government soldiers. The villagers got caught in the middle.

The more the government represses the population, the better off each individual member of the community is supporting the insurrection. This works in favor of the rebels, who can offer protection to potential victims in return for support for the rebellion.

The recent uptick in the killing of civilians in Afghanistan is a contemporary example of how government responses can facilitate rebel recruitment. U.S. and NATO forces bomb civilian targets, either intentionally on suspicion of the presence of combatants within the civilian population or mistakenly. Either way, civilians are traumatized and feel less and less secure, fearful of seemingly random acts of violence perpetrated against them. When a wedding party is strafed, a family compound bombed; when violence is visited upon them even when they are not in the rebel camp, they must look for protection from elsewhere. The rebels can provide that protection, and all they will ask for in return is support—information, weapons storage, food and lodging, hideouts. When the two are sides split more clearly—as they would be in the midst of a civil war without an outside party being involved in the random violence—it is easier to identify the source of the gravest threat and find protection in the most reliable ally.

The repression meted out by the government, moreover, targets specific groups of people, in particular those of identifiable religious, ethnic, or social categories; members of specific villages that are suspected of supporting rebels; and families of rebel soldiers. Union organizers fighting for better wages and working conditions, and ethnic minorities who are discriminated against politically and economically, are also primary targets. At some point in the level of repression—when torture, killings, and imprisonment become so widespread as to be unavoidable—people will turn to the rebels for protection.

After that long bus ride in the mountains in Guatemala, many hours of conversation about the insurgency, its social and political costs, and prospects for victory, my friend arranged for me to meet with a group of dissidents. Surreal detours and mysterious twists and turns through city streets ended at a nondescript door in Guatemala City. When we knocked, the curtains covering the window moved ever so slightly, the door cracked open the slightest. My friend exchanged a few words with an unseen person on the other side. The door closed. We waited. A few minutes later I was handed a sheet of paper with an address and directions. At the end of another convoluted journey with many bus changes, I found myself in a middle-class neighborhood in the city, knocking on the door of a house like all the others in the area. Inside this one, however, was a meeting of the executive council of Grupo de Apoyo Mutuo (GAM)—the "mutual support group for mothers of the disappeared." This was a support group for people who lost friends or family to the repressive government, but beyond mutual support, it was also one of the primary organizing tools of the opposition. The GAM council was planning a march on the president's house, and they asked that I participate. They felt the government would be less likely to use violence if an American was present. By the end of the afternoon I had agreed to participate, though I was neither convinced of the logic of their argument nor completely comfortable engaging in political protest in a foreign country in the midst of civil war. I left the house with a list of hundreds of names of people recently "disappeared" by the government, which the GAM council wanted me to take back home. In spite of my trepidation I did participate in the march. The experience left me with the question of why these people would choose this path, when on an average day of protest they would be beaten, arrested, or at worst "disappeared," never to be heard from again; where their best defense against abuse—or death—was a single American. The question of how it came to this, where a simple desire for a fairer share in your country's wealth could result in a very real fear of death at the hands of your own government.

It was the political process that had failed. The same political process that determined the distribution of political and economic resources, that contributed to the motivation to rebel, that provided incentives for the opposition to overcome the problem of collective action. On the road to civil war, this is another milestone—a different government response to early political demands would steer the process in a different, and better, direction.

9

♦ ♦ ♦

INTRANSIGENCE AND REPRESSION

The military dictatorship that ruled Argentina from 1976 to 1983 was one of the more repressive and ruthless governments in the world. Although it is difficult to know the exact figure, estimates of the number of people killed by this regime approach thirty thousand. The methods used were diabolical, almost impossible to believe. People were kidnapped, put in internment camps, tortured, murdered. Men and women were thrown from airplanes into the ocean, bound and alive, never surfacing, never seen again. The details of such deeds sometimes come to light long after victims and even perpetrators of these violations are dead and the regime has ended. Apart from incredulity and horror that specific events generate, there are questions that arise about why governments act in these ways, in spite of international law, in spite of clear norms against such violations.

Governments use repression against groups because it is effective, at least in the short term. It is the politics of fear, the effort to instill terror in those who might be persuaded to act in support of the opposition. Governments make the mistake of thinking of their own citizens as opposition, as threats, even as terrorists, when they are, at least in the beginning, no more than disgruntled people drawing attention to their situation, protesting policies that hurt them.

Many of us, as concerned citizens, have written letters, signed petitions, attended meetings, or even marched in political rallies or demonstrations. All these are forms of political protest, and are usually low-risk, nonviolent actions. Opposition organizations first try the nonviolent approach to voice dissent; violence is usually the last resort. It is puzzling, therefore, that a government facing organized protesters doesn't take steps to placate them. If political leaders thought they could end up fighting a civil war, they might try accommodation first.

Policies of repression are choices that leaders make. They could, instead, choose conciliatory policies that work toward concessions. Rebel leaders also face this choice of whether or not to use repression, but usually only after a civil war has started. Government leaders, however, have to decide their response to the initial demands of the opposition, and it is this choice that can profoundly impact the future course of events.

Consider this from the perspective of governments, which see themselves as legitimate representatives of the majority. Leaders pass laws that impose restrictions on people in their community. These might result in a subsidy reduction, new policies with regard to landholdings, or new taxes that hurt the poor disproportionately. They choose to make these new laws willingly and after considerable thought. They have a constituency to consider, one that is probably pushing them toward these new policies. Even in the United States it is easy to see laws passed that appear to benefit certain groups over others. In small and poor countries these issues are exacerbated. The industrial sector may demand banning of labor unions, the urban elite may want to tax the rural sector, or the IMF demands economic reforms that require reduction in subsidies. Whatever the source of these political changes advocated by political insiders or the opposition, there will be one group of people supporting them and another opposing them. It is often easier for those in power to ignore minority or weaker groups that are hit harder by their policies. Political repression will follow the pattern that exclusion did, completing the picture of group polarization in the process of civil wars. It is not identity, religious or ethnic, that provokes this targeted response, but the fact of political opposition and the threat that any opposition, even peaceful, implies to those in power.

Repression is part of the civil war process. It is a strategy that sometimes works to stifle opposition, but often it is state violence itself that is responsible for pushing the opposition from nonviolent dissent toward armed rebellion. Many—too many—governments choose to respond with violence instead of accommodating the demands of disenfranchised citizens. The tragedy is that they generally have other options that could minimize armed resistance in the short term and achieve a more stable political environment in the long term. It is odd, but a government almost has to try hard to generate conditions that benefit rebel leaders. Accommodation by the government to demands of the opposition work against a rebel leader attempting to recruit rebel soldiers. If, however, a government responds too violently and too indiscriminately, there is greater incentive for an individual to join with the rebels in an attempt to seek protection from the government. The terror of political repression, that is, acts as a recruiting tool for the rebel army. The evidence demonstrates that violence begets violence. In 1972, the killing of thirteen demonstrators by the British—Bloody Sunday—touched off the next thirty years of the struggles in Northern Ireland. In 1976, government repression and the beating death of Steven Biko in Soweto, South Africa, mobilized the black townships into open dissent. Today, throughout the Muslim world, violent suppression of dissent appears to be turning many toward violent responses. Even where a compromise may have been possible, the resort to repression begins to cut off alternatives.

How does a government repress opposition groups? It might start with arrests and interrogations of leaders at a demonstration. It is easy to find out who they are, and hauling them into the police station for some stern warnings may be enough to intimidate them into backing down. What I witnessed in Bangladesh was the security apparatus of the government clamping down hard on the organizers of the protest. Protest movements in the United States during the 1960s and 1970s faced harsh responses. The Kent State University killings took it to the extreme, but there were many other instances of efforts to stifle protests. The infamous "red files" describe actions of repression and surveillance by U.S. authorities of people and organizations deemed a threat to political stability. As the number and frequency of protests accelerate, a government begins to feel increasingly threatened and finds itself in a conundrum: If it accedes to the demands of the opposition, it appears weak to its primary supporters. But if it uses increasingly abusive methods against detractors, it risks turning a nonviolent movement into a violent one. It is at this point, when passive protest is answered with brutality, that opposition groups begin to think about an armed struggle as an alternative to the normal political process. And it is at this point governments cross the Rubicon into internal warfare.

When faced with the prospect of being arrested, beaten, tortured, even killed by your government, the notion of joining a group trying to shoot its way into power can be very intimidating. Quite often, those who were tortured and killed are left on the side of the road, or some place in public view, to warn people thinking about cooperating with the opposition to think again. After watching the treatment of the protesters in Bangladesh, I felt an acute distaste for the violence, and feared for my own physical integrity. It was suddenly very easy for me to see why the number of people supporting the rebels was so small. This combination of brutality, reports from those who have been arrested and released, rumors, disappearances, evidence of dead rebels, and people's imagination adds up to an atmosphere of dread. Fear for your own or your family's safety and lives is a powerful deterrent.

If the government can create just enough fear, but not too much, then people might conclude that the cost of rebellion is too high. But if the government goes overboard and the repression begins to look either entirely random, or as if any individual is nearly certain to be raped, dismembered, shot, or dropped into the sea simply because of who he is, then joining the insurgency will look like a much better strategy. Under these conditions armed rebels can offer protection from the arbitrary violence of the government. In return the rebels would expect loyalty and support for the rebel movement. Joining with rebels is a risk, but not doing so could be worse. The sight of one mutilated body might be the push over the edge. There are no easy choices in such a situation, but fear forces people to make one.

The term *disappeared*, in Guatemala as in Argentina, is used to describe opponents of the government who were abducted and never heard from again. We learn, sometimes years later, of what was done to these people in the name of fighting communism or for political stability or national security. The names on the list GAM gave me were brothers, sisters, mothers, fathers, all of whom were somehow linked to the opposition. Their families had no trace of them, no information, just the awful assumption of what had happened. This form of repression was systemic in Guatemala. My list contained at least two hundred names and I was given this list at a time when the United States was reporting a dramatic decline in the number of disappeared persons and, on that basis, increasing aid to the Guatemalan government. In fact GAM gave me the list hoping I would help counter the U.S. story that "disappearance" was no longer a method prevalent on the Guatemalan political scene.

It terrified me to be holding that list. I was afraid to leave it in my hotel room, afraid to carry it on my person. I was convinced the police had access to my room, and certain that they could have stopped me at any time. If they found it I would end up, at best, jailed for supporting revolutionaries. I couldn't bring myself to throw the list away; I felt I owed it to the people at GAM to take it out of the country. It seems hard to believe today, but I carried that stack of papers everywhere with me for a week thinking the military would be less likely to search me than my room, and I eventually threw it away before I crossed the border into Honduras. Getting caught with that list and being jailed or tortured was not something I thought I could endure. I wasn't part of their movement, just trying to learn about it, but holding on to that list for only a week gave me a small window onto the fear those opposition leaders must have felt every single day. I learned firsthand the psychological toll supporting rebels or challenging the government must take, and I also experienced the fear that repression can root in an individual.

The U.S. government reported in 2002 that up to forty thousand Guatemalans were "disappeared" during the civil war. The population of Guatemala is around ten million. Forty thousand people translates into one in every two hundred and fifty people gone without a trace. If that level of terror were waged in the United States it would result in a million people vanishing, leaving families and friends with no knowledge of whether they were dead or being held incommunicado. This is equivalent to the entire population of Dallas, the population of Denver twice over, or my hometown twenty times over. It is staggering to think of this level of impunity. I was scared out of my wits I might become one of those people on that list I was burdened with, one insignificant person in the scheme of things, if I actually got caught with it. I didn't have the courage of conviction required of those people who confronted their government on a daily basis. In the face of such horrible and systematic abuse the fear is unrelenting, and I got rid of that list and felt bad for doing so.

If acceptable standards of human rights are so important, why didn't the United States cut off aid to Guatemala? National interest is the primary—though vague—explanation. What it implies is that governments will ignore each other's use of repression against political opponents as long as it is not overtly visible and is in rough parity with the level of threat they face. In short, repression is used and can work, yet most countries would denounce it quickly if called on to do so. It will be denounced as a general policy but ignored in specific instances. Most political leaders seem to recognize that leadership comes with the risk of having to confront a committed opposition, and that repression is one of the mechanisms for maintaining stability. Repression is something no government would dismiss categorically. This is in part why the Bush administration was so willing to use torture against Iraqi and Afghani prisoners, all the while denouncing torture as barbaric.

Political repression is not confined to the most notorious governments or brutal dictators. It is like an insidious disease that afflicts most governments. The United States overthrew Saddam Hussein, ostensibly because of the potential threat of his military power, but also because he was a brutal leader. In the months following his overthrow, the United States itself became a brutal occupier. Even the United States, which heralds itself as the champion of human rights and democracy, fell victim to the ease and impunity with which governments can use repressive tactics to stifle dissent. Governments that feel threatened rely on repression because they have mechanisms in place that make it easy for them to imprison, torture, and kill, but also because repression often works.

Amnesty International and the U.S. Department of State each publish an annual report on human rights records of countries around the world. These reports detail, among other things, the amount of political repression reported in each country. The State Department's report covers well over three thousand pages, giving a good sense of how governments respond to challenges from within their own borders. Even the names of the categories point to how brutal governments can be in defense of their right to rule. For example, the State Department reports on what are called "physical integrity of person" indicators, which includes an evaluation of whether a government uses political detention, arbitrary imprisonment, torture, kidnapping, and killings as forms of political control.

In spite of having all the mechanisms in place to be able to torture and kill their own, almost all governments have signed agreements not to do this. Repression builds suspicion and resentment, and ultimately it takes the suppression of humanity to torture and murder people. For a government, repressing citizens is a drastic undertaking, even compared to the prospect of losing power. Even so, evidence shows that repression usually starts before there is any serious hint of an armed rebellion. Many leaders adopt repressive policies as a normal part of running a government, albeit policies they prefer, as far as possible, to keep hidden from the world. Since most political leaders feel at least a little threatened by the existence of or demands from a disenfranchised minority group, they are reluctant to speak out against the use of political repression. This is what makes U.S. behavior appear so odd, and the State Department's annual report on human rights practices around the world so valuable, for understanding the prevalence of repression. On the one hand the Bush administration was a vocal champion of human rights. On the other, it condoned the torture of political prisoners. Concessions are always an option, regardless of the type of government. Committing to land reform, permitting unions, allowing local languages and customs—are all ways to pacify aggrieved groups. Even though repression is such a drastic step, governments do not always choose other, more pacific strategies. The State Department reports attest to this fact.

Consider for a moment that repression is a legitimate tool for controlling a population, particularly in response to actions of a specific group fundamentally opposed to government policy. Think of the effect mutilated corpses just outside a village or on the main street in your town would have, and the "value" of repression will come to light. International laws and accepted norms of behavior make it clear that torture, arbitrary imprisonment, and any form of government abuse are unacceptable ways to treat citizens, to treat people. And yet, most governments engage in these behaviors at some time and at some level. Their defense is often that they have no other choice, that the threat they face warrants extreme measures. In effect, self-exoneration based on the level of threat. This is what the United States claims in defense of its treatment of prisoners at Guantánamo, Cuba, and Abu Ghraib, Iraq, and the other rendition prisons around the world. The argument is, if sufficiently threatened, governments should be able to respond with their own version of terror. Israel makes this claim as justification for its response to Palestinians; the United States uses this justification in its struggles with the insurgencies in Iraq and Afghanistan. What it means to be sufficiently threatened is quite subjective; at the worst the existence of an opposition group will be all it takes; at the other extreme it can be the belief that a group is committed to overthrowing the government.

In Bangladesh, I was a last-minute add-on to a dinner party at the home of an employee of the U.S. Agency for International Development (USAID). I found myself seated next to the first secretary at the Pakistani mission there. I had not the diplomatic credentials of the other guests. I ventured to ask the man undiplomatically about three men I had met a few days before in Calcutta, and about Pakistani policy with regard to political opposition. These three men I spoke of had been staying in my hostel in Calcutta after having been released from a Pakistani prison. They were political dissidents, part of a prodemocracy group advocating for political access and a new distribution of political power. They had described the torture and abuse they suffered as political prisoners. The diplomat was puzzled by my question, but after a brief consultation in Urdu with his wife, he said, "Oh, I know the party to which you refer. We recently shot a number of them. We think the problem is no longer important." It was cold and callous and reflected the political realities of the time.

I no longer recall whether the men I met were part of the Baloch nationalist movement or responding to the coup that brought General Zia ul-Haq to power. What does remain in my memory is the incredulousness of those three men at their treatment, and the callousness I saw in the representative of their government. The government, at least as represented by that diplomat, appeared to have no idea about the demands of the opposition, their view of the status quo, or any sense that they posed a real threat to the government's authority. It is that callousness, that general disregard for what are often legitimate demands and legitimate protests, that leads directly to the opposition taking up arms.

At the core, it is those people who threaten the interests of governments who are targeted. Many governments have a shaky hold on power to start with. Many leaders live perpetually under threat of a coup or military takeover, and any demands by the opposition only increase this sense of insecurity. If there are not sufficiently strong political institutions within a country, there might not really be ways to meet the competing demands of the two groups, the political elite and the opposition. If the government lets the protests and rallies get too far out of hand, it will be challenged by its own supporters. But if it begins to repress the opposition, the opposition groups begin to run out of options. In far too many cases the leader of the government adopts a repressive response, because at the time it may be easier than making concessions, and there is a real possibility it could work. That is at least what evidence tells us—repression works to stifle protest at the same time it pushes opposition groups toward armed rebellion. Repression becomes a tool of control over political opponents because governments don't want to fall. Political leaders cherish their political survival. Some desire the wealth that comes with power; some think their policies are best for their people. Whatever their motivation to avoid concessions, they turn to the tools of government that can be most effective. The problem is that it is a two-edged sword.

It doesn't take a great leap of imagination to think that anyone who participates in the seditious act of joining an armed rebellion poses a serious threat to the government, and therefore the government is going to make life very difficult for any of those people they apprehend. In many cases even people in the villages of rebel leaders are subject to torture and other abuses at the hands of authorities. Israel, for instance, demolishes homes of families from which its attackers come, using collective punishment as a deterrence to prevent further attacks. From a government's perspective they want to make it very costly for a person thinking about joining a rebellion to make that choice. Government soldiers have wiped out many villages around the world in an effort to demonstrate this point. Under such conditions joining with rebels is a perilous choice. Still, it happens all the time. To build a rebel insurgency that has even a slim chance of success, rebel leaders have to convince individuals to risk everything on the chance for a change. The government, at the same time, must try to make that choice as difficult as possible. The fear instilled by repression is one way to do this.

I began by talking about how poverty is at the heart of most civil wars. Most poor countries, though, are not fighting civil wars. Part of the reason for this is the extreme risk to individuals who oppose the government. Even poverty, disillusionment, and lack of hope fall short of the conditions required for an individual to take up arms to change policies that created the situation. A civil war is the endgame in the process of making demands that has gone wrong on multiple dimensions. Poverty plays a role at many critical points in the process. To start with, poverty contributes to the motivation to protest policies of the government. Without some sort of grievance any one individual would lack the motivation to take the next set of steps, particularly as each step becomes increasingly risky. There are many ways in which a low level of national wealth leaves the margins too tight for many individuals. Even small economic changes can lead to dramatic changes in the level of motivation to protest or rebel. But poor countries tend to have few options with which to respond to political challenges. When a country is poor—and most of those fighting civil wars in 2002 were poor—there is little left in the treasury to distribute. The pie is too small and not growing fast enough. If leaders take from one constituency to give to another, their next challenge is already in the making.

Poor countries also tend to have a poorly developed infrastructure, which helps rebel leaders organize a rebellion. If there is no good road system into far reaches of a province or jungle, it allows a budding rebel army to find easy sanctuary. One advantage of an organized military is the ability to move troops rapidly. But an underdeveloped infrastructure takes away some of the military's advantages over rebels. Rebels have an easier time avoiding detection as they plan their next attack. Each of these factors works in favor of armed insurrections. To effectively fight a government, however, rebels need weapons that pose at least a minimal challenge to government troops. The poorer rebels are, the less likely it is that they can generate the resources to outfit anything but a meager army. So poverty works both sides of the street.

Given the economic conditions that provide the material motivations to challenge the government, group cohesion helps facilitate the process of organizing people for the task. But there still needs to be that critical force that will compel any one individual to take the step of siding with the opposition over the government. The government often provides it by responding with brutality and repression to demands of certain members of its population. Without targeted discrimination and targeted repression, the chances of organizing a rebellion would decline dramatically. The chances of civil war would also decline dramatically.

10

♦ ♦ ♦

SCYLLA AND CHARYBDIS

One of the resistance fighters I met in Palestine, a young man in his twenties, had been shot in the head by Israeli forces. His head was deformed from that encounter with the rubber bullet they had used; it took him a year in the hospital to recover from the injury. He had been ten years old at the time.

Every life is unique, but this life also serves as an example. It contains elements common to all civil wars: There is the awful brutality that disregards norms of humanity and rules of warfare—a child being shot in the head is hard to accept, even in times of war. Outside this man's door there is the refugee camp, rampant with the conditions that spawn civil wars the world over. And inside, the man at the end of that road, hopeless and trapped in a situation he believes will change only if he changes it—by force and by risking his life to do so.

Individuals participate in insurgencies in a bid to change their lot. Civil wars are an attempt to change conditions that are no longer tolerable. We can think of civil wars in terms of their consequences: the consequences of a war, and the consequences if one does not take place. The consequences of war are many and horrific, a catalog of trauma and death. But we must also consider the consequences of not having a war, in the sense of the persistence of protracted misery, stemming from poverty, neglect, and abuse, that so many endure for generations.

Living in a wealthy industrialized country, it is perhaps difficult to imagine conditions that could spawn a civil war. But for many, many people these are not abstract conditions. People suffer terribly, in very real ways, every single day of their lives. Forty-seven countries were listed by the UN as having per capita incomes of less than $500 per year in 2002, representing nearly one-quarter of all the world's countries. The average individual in the thirty-five wealthiest countries has more than twenty times the income of a person in these poorer countries, as much as eighty times the income on the extreme end of the spectrum.

There is, however, little merit in focusing on how much rich countries have compared to poor ones. Poor countries do have their share of wealthy people, and any one poor country could reduce its poverty greatly were resources distributed more equitably. The simplest solution might be to distribute political influence differently. But rarely do political leaders voluntarily relinquish power. This is at the crux of what makes people rise up against their government. Rebellions might not change these skewed distributions or increase national wealth dramatically, but they do represent one form of political pressure that can influence those making policies.

One of the primary tools of the UN Development Program is the Human Development Index (HDI). The indicators used to generate the HDI include life expectancy, income, and access to education, and by combining data on these indicators the HDI attempts to capture the quality of life of the average person living in each country. It is possible to compare countries over time and with each other—observing progress relative to how it was doing the year before, or relative to other countries. As just one example of how hard life is for some people, of the twenty-five lowest-ranked countries on the HDI, twenty-one have life expectancies of less than fifty years. There are nine countries in the world in which the average life expectancy of a baby born in 2002 is under forty years, and in the country lowest on the list it is just under thirty-three years. A child born today in Canada can expect to live to eighty, while one born in Zambia can only expect to live to thirty-two. (A description of these data is at the end of the book.)

The independent effect of poverty is a factor in this distressingly low life expectancy. Poverty means a harder life, more disease, and less medical care. Life on the edge of survival exacts a toll on many dimensions, and access to medical care is just one of them. There can be little doubt, too, that life expectancy in poor countries is low because of the AIDS epidemic. AIDS is ravaging Africa and spreading rapidly in Asia. Ninety-five percent of people with AIDS live in developing countries, and by far most AIDS-related deaths occur in these countries. Although there has been a dramatic decline in the rate of AIDS-related deaths in industrialized countries, lack of access to medical treatment means it is only accelerating in the poorer countries. Poverty accounts for a large part of the reason why treatment is not universally available.

Twenty-five thousand people die every day from hunger or hunger-related complications. At this rate my entire hometown would be lost to hunger and malnutrition in a single day. A city the size of Detroit would be decimated in a month. Conditions of extreme poverty are also conditions of short life expectancy. And if a country is so poor that poverty holds sway over the population, it is likely the education system is broken. Data from the UNDP confirm this, and also show that women are generally underrepresented in education enrollments. And it is not an accident, either, that these are the countries more likely to find themselves embroiled in a civil war. Even when people know the potential horrors of war and the possibility of defeat, the conditions they live under are sometimes enough to compel them to violence. The price they pay for rebellion could well be high, but so too is the price they pay for living in those conditions.

Civil wars are different from international wars, and civil wars, unlike international wars, follow no rules of warfare. The adage "war is hell" may in fact not be forceful enough to describe civil wars.

International wars have rules. There is a stated purpose. There is a strategy by which to achieve that purpose, which is followed by generals in pursuit of that purpose. It is quite often in civil wars that we read about the atrocities that get etched into our collective memories.

Children are soldiers, rape is a weapon, killing is indiscriminate. No one and nothing is exempt from the brutality. Afghanistan, Iraq, Rwanda, Sudan, and the Congo have civil wars in the public eye today, and many of the other civil wars are just as brutal as these more publicly visible ones, even though the casualty list may not be as long.

We usually describe wars in terms of numbers of people killed—body counts are what people remember most. That, and major battles of a war. In the United States we remember Gettysburg, Fort Sumter, Iwo Jima, Bunker Hill, Normandy, and Tet. Soldiers maimed, generations lost, and treasuries depleted are lost to collective memory with the passage of time. World War I stuck in my grandmother's mind as the "great war" perhaps because it caused so many casualties. She spoke of the magnitude of the carnage above all else. Millions of people died in those four years of warfare. She never called the Second World War the "great war" even though many more people were killed, even though she had a son who fought in that war. The numbers, perhaps, were so staggering that it was beyond her willingness to consider yet another war that big. The point is that we tend to remember how many people died, particularly on "our" side of the war.

Death is a tragic part of war, whether civil or international. The line between civil and international wars is often indistinct. The Vietnam War started as a civil war. The United States got involved in all the wrong ways, at a cost of about fifty-eight thousand of "our" soldiers. The number of Vietnamese killed gets lost in our memories and in our textbooks, as do other gruesome aspects of that war, but that number of our own dead remains in our minds. Whatever else you might think of the Iraq war, it too had an overwhelming flavor of civil war until the invasion of 2003. Torture and abuse were rampant, as were the use of chemical gases and military campaigns of intimidation and extermination. The U.S. invasion initially transformed that conflict into an international one. And the horrors of war have persisted unabated. Pervasive fear of mistreatment or worse from a dictator's military has given way to fear of bombings, imprisonment, and random violence from the occupation and those fighting it. By 2006 the foreign policy establishment caught up with conventional wisdom to recognize that once again Iraq is in the midst of a civil war, and that the United States is caught right in the middle of it. The United States will eventually build a war memorial to the soldiers who have died in Iraq, even if we never fully understand why they were there.

Civil wars kill and maim an awful lot of people, young, old, men, women, military, civilian. About thirty thousand American soldiers died in the Korean War, about two hundred and fifty thousand in World War II, one hundred fifteen thousand in the First World War, five hundred fifty thousand in the American Civil War. The Civil War was twice as deadly as World War II in terms of casualties. When you consider that the population of the United States during the Civil War was a hundred million less than during World War II, you get a sense of just how bloody the American Civil War was. The Rwandan civil war and the massacre that followed killed a million or so people. As a statistic this number is shocking in itself. But when you consider that the population of Rwanda was 7 million at the time, the million dead represented one-seventh of the total population of the country. One-seventh of the population was wiped out in a spasm of violence that lasted three months. Reports of up to two hundred and fifty thousand people dying in the Bosnian conflict led to the NATO intervention in 1994. The civil war that began in Somalia in 1991 left about three hundred thousand dead. There was the Cambodian conflict of the mid-1970s. It is very clear that huge numbers of people die struggling for change in their political, social, and economic lives. Not all of them are willing victims. Some get caught in the crossfire, or are used as pawns to get at the other side's military. Today we witness unimaginably brutal fighting among groups vying for power in the Democratic Republic of the Congo (DRC). The International Rescue Committee reports that three million people have been killed since the outbreak of civil war in 1998, with intermittent spasms of violence that would boggle the mind.

The cost of civil wars, though, cannot be counted only in terms of the dead. On October 26, 2004, the *New York Times* reported that forty thousand women and girls were raped during six years of civil war in the Congo. Rape is a horrendous crime under any circumstances, but when used as a political tool it takes on particularly inhumane dimensions. Men are forced to watch the repeated gang rape of their mothers, sisters, wives, and daughters, a technique to extract information from them. In pursuit of the aims of war, it is a violation of the entire society. It puts war almost beyond belief, but it can and does play out in these ways. The Congo is not alone; it is happening in Darfur as I write. The Serbs carried out similar policies of systematic rape in Kosovo in 1998.

A report by the World Bank, *Breaking the Conflict Trap,* points out how and why civil wars push countries further into financial ruin. Investment becomes too great a risk in a country at war with itself. The role of the World Bank is to lend money to help countries develop their economic and social infrastructure, but civil wars make countries most in need of World Bank support bad risks. Outside capital dries up because of political instability. An unstable country also causes local capital to be invested in foreign countries. Even if the government it supports wins the war, the wrecked economy makes it more difficult for capital to generate acceptable returns, if at all. Economic elites in an unstable country always run the risk of their government losing and their businesses, land, and financial reserves being swept up in changes instituted by victorious rebels. They will therefore move their money to some other country, maybe to a place they can flee to if the rebels are on the verge of victory. Many of these countries are very poor to start with, and when external investment dries up and internal money flees the country, the government is left with very little room to maneuver. When faced with an armed rebellion demanding changes, these governments have very little capacity to make accommodations, even if they wanted to.

In long-running civil wars countries are left with the lost children of war. In Northern Ireland, the Occupied Territories of Palestine, and Sri Lanka, to name but a few, sometimes they have little opportunity for education or to develop the skills to work; sometimes the psychological trauma of war turns many children into aspiring martyrs. Israeli and Palestinian children confront this dilemma, as do child soldiers in Africa. I grew up thinking I would be a doctor, lawyer, president, or scientist. I cannot imagine being willing to die for independence, strapping a bomb to myself to free my people at age twelve or thirteen. How do you ever go back to school after having once considered martyrdom? Entire generations of children grow up knowing nothing but warfare, abuse, destruction, and death, and are left without education, without hope, without expectations for the future.

At the end of a war, society must rebuild, and to do so effectively requires manpower and resources. Recent studies have shown that countries that fight civil wars often get caught up in another war soon after the first ends. People turn to types of behavior they know best, so the end of a civil war does not always mean the end of all civil wars in that country, or even a period of peace long enough to rebuild their shattered society. Often our focus is on the more brutal aspects of civil wars—murder, rape, refugees—but the long-term consequences might be even more difficult to contend with. The effects of civil wars continue long after the abominations that people witness during the course of a war fade away. Far from achieving the goals and hopes of those who signed up for a better future, the process of fighting a civil war contributes to a whole host of events that, like residual radiation from radioactive fallout, continues to adversely affect an already traumatized population and depleted treasury.

One of the more visible aspects of civil war is the large migration of people who are uprooted and become part of a human wave escaping dangers awaiting them in their homes, communities, or villages. You might remember BBC reports of mass refugee flows into feeding centers in Ethiopia in the early 1980s. Huge numbers of people barely limped into refugee camps looking for food and shelter. Many died along the roadside. The scenes were heartbreaking. The U.S. and NATO intervention in Kosovo in 1999 was largely driven by the spectacle of hundreds of thousands of Albanians fleeing abuse at the hands of Serbs. The United Nations High Commission for Refugees (UNHCR) estimated that one million people left Kosovo for refugee camps in neighboring countries. Those who stayed or did not get out fast enough faced systematic abuse—gang rapes, executions of men and boys. But it was mass movements of hungry, frightened, abused people that forced the world's attention. In Iraq today it is estimated that there are three and a half million refugees out of a total population of twenty-two million.

There is compelling evidence showing governments are much more likely to respond only after the consequences of war become too difficult to ignore. Massive refugee flows are one of those human tragedies that are hard to hide. When people flee their homes they have to go somewhere, and that "somewhere" is most often a neighboring country. The humanitarian response to such flows of people is to set up refugee centers, which brings more people and with them more visibility. The media follows the flow of hungry people with horrific stories to tell. At some point the problem becomes a global issue and the United Nations, donor countries, and private volunteer organizations have to get involved. The civil war might be the problem, but the refugee crisis and the human tragedy are the symptoms that must be addressed.

The United Nations High Commission for Refugees exists to look after and help resettle refugees from around the world. In 2002 the UNHCR reported that there were just over fifteen million internally displaced and external refugees being sheltered around the world. The difference in the type of refugee depends on whether a person seeks shelter within her own country or flees to a different one. From the point of view of refugees this may be a distinction without much meaning. In either case they leave their homes, jobs, and most of what they cherish for the bleak conditions of a camp. According to the U.S. Census Bureau, in 2002 there were 193 countries in the world, and only 60 of these countries have populations greater than fifteen million. The number of people living in refugee camps, then, represents a number greater than the population of nearly 70 percent of all the countries in the world. In fact the number of refugees is about double the population of Switzerland or Israel. Most of these people have left their homes to escape a civil war, and collectively they represent a huge cost from civil wars for the world community to deal with.

The cost of fighting a civil war, even a brief one, is very high, and there is as yet no convincing evidence that civil wars work to reverse existing conditions for the majority of people. For me to make the claim that civil wars are useful I would have to make a case that rebellions lead to changes in levels of misery, because either new leadership takes a different policy approach or negotiated settlements are able to address some of the economic and political distribution issues that led to the conflict. The difficulty is that you have to weigh real human costs of a civil war against struggles of life at the margins. The real question is how to weigh the cost of a rebel soldier who dies young fighting for change against the person who dies young because of his living conditions. It is tricky, but there is a way to get a sense of the effectiveness of civil wars.

Using data collected by the Correlates of War Project at the University of Michigan on the ending of civil wars, and the UNDP data on the Human Development Index, we can get a sense of how effective civil wars can be. Remember, the Human Development Index is a measure of the quality of life for an average individual within a country. If civil wars actually make things better, this should show up as a higher ranking on the HDI after the conclusion of a war. This change in the HDI score should be particularly evident if the war was won by the rebels or ended through negotiations. The UNDP provides a ranking of countries at five-year intervals from 1975 through 2000. For example, Norway, Sweden, Canada, and Australia tend to rank in the top four over the past twenty-five years, the United States consistently in the top ten. This index goes back only as far as 1975, but it does provide enough coverage to get a sense of whether things get better after a civil war. If a government won, it would have very little reason to give in to the demands of the rebels. If the rebels won, they would have every reason to make good on promises they made to recruits. A negotiated settlement should also lead to changes more in line with the rebels' position, or else fighting would have continued.

The data give us a snapshot of the outcome from civil wars that started between 1980 and 1990 and ended by 1995. There are many more civil wars that happen outside of this period, but in order to have HDI data before and after the war, I'm constrained. This provides an HDI score for at least one period before the war and at least one after it ended. If results point to dramatically better conditions, we could consider the positive impact of civil wars on people's quality of life.

Civil War Outcomes and Human Development

	Number of Outcomes	Better HDI in the Postconflict Period	Worse HDI in the Postconflict Period
Agreement or Negotiated Settlement	2	2	0
Government Victory	10	5	5
Opposition Victory	3	2	1

Note: There were nine other conflicts that started and ended in this period for which HDI data were not available either for the beginning or the end of the conflict.

The table, which shows cases for which data are available, is easily summarized by saying that the outcome of a civil war is a bit of a crap shoot. In nine of the fifteen countries for which I have data during this period, the quality of life was better after the war than before. One interpretation is that civil wars result in political changes that translate into changes in life conditions. But the government wins about two-thirds of the time, and only in half of those government victories does the quality of life conditions change for the better. Rebels appear to win only about 20 percent of the wars and in two-thirds of these the outcome looks better after the war than before. As with most social conditions, data are missing for six countries that fought and ended wars during this fifteen-year period, but the general trend is evident. The government wins more than it loses, and in more than half the wars the HDI ranking improves within five years of the end of the war.

The question is whether it takes a civil war to end the structural conditions that create poverty for an individual living at the margins. The answer is clearly no. Countries give up their treasury, their youth, and so many of their people when they fail to make the political accommodations that could prevent a civil war. The trauma of civil war is endured needlessly, but the poor of these countries do not carry the political clout to compel changes through peaceful means, so rebellion becomes their primary option.

There are not a lot of good options here. The conditions that many in the world experience are enough to make your skin crawl, and certainly enough to make some individuals choose to join a rebellion. I cannot say which I would choose: unacceptable compliance and life— or death—as a rebel. The conditions that lead to civil wars—poverty, discrimination, and despair—are so common that it is not hard to understand why people conclude that change is warranted and necessary. But the method of making changes looks a lot worse than riding out those terrible conditions. Illness, disease, and death are all part of life. Starvation is a dreadful way to die, but it happens with some regularity. I spent some weeks working in the Home for the Destitute and Dying in Calcutta, India. This is the place Mother Teresa of the Missionaries of Charity made famous for her work with the poorest of the poor. In my short time there I tended to dozens of people who were in the process of starving to death. Their last days were spent in humane conditions, but the conditions that got them to the doorstep of the Home could not have been good. Starvation looked to me like a gruesome way to die. The body withers away, and eventually gets to a point where efforts to revive it are futile. Moving people into and out of the limited number of beds was regular and systematic. There were enough people starving to death in Calcutta that there was never a vacancy. Those who made it to the Home were the lucky ones, and they usually died within days.

The alternative is to take the risks associated with forcing change. When you take the costs of all that happens in civil wars into account, fighting for change seems a bleak strategy. When people are hungry they don't also suffer the indignity of rape. When life expectancy is short and wage labor nonexistent, there is no risk of torture or imprisonment. And hunger and malnutrition can be addressed more effectively outside of refugee camps. So the immense cost of fighting civil wars should lead to policies that prevent their necessity or reduce their consequences if they do start. These are clearly political problems requiring political solutions, and if the political will existed these things could be changed. But poor countries tend to have fewer choices when faced with political demands, so the leadership will take the path of least resistance. Typically that works against opportunity for redress for the poor.

The choice for them is between Scylla and Charybdis—the monsters Odysseus encountered—where even careful navigation is fraught with risks; steering away from one finds you too close to the other. The choice is between living in conditions that are no longer acceptable and fighting a war that rarely brings redemption.

The necessary changes should be possible without the violence of war, and could be advanced with coherent and targeted policies implemented by the wealthier countries of the world. If conditions that lead people to rise up against their governments never change, then we will continually confront the scourge of civil war.

Given the ideology of the day, I harbor no expectations that the collective will of the world community will act to end hunger and despair across the globe. Poverty will be left to the marketplace, and those who cannot compete will be left out. As my father once told me, there will be many more civil wars and rebellions to come. Once they do, however, there are ways for the global village to get involved and, I believe, to shorten the length of most civil wars and mitigate some of the consequences.

WORLD STAGE

11

◆ ◆ ◆

LAWYERS, GUNS,
AND MONEY

December of 2006, I waited in a hotel room in Ramallah for a phone call that would set up a meeting that might lead to another meeting. This was what I was in Palestine for, against the advice of friends and family. The wait was long, and for the most part boring, interspersed with moments of anxiety and doubt about my own sanity. I thought about the fact that, in spite of half a century of peace talks, accords, cease-fires, and UN resolutions, this conflict endures. There is still an armed resistance in Palestine, and I was about to meet them.

Understanding the conditions and motivations that find regular people fighting in civil wars does not provide us with a way out of the war. Victory or defeat is definitive closure, but any other outcomes are fraught with pitfalls. Once a war is being fought, there is a profound erosion of trust and an abundance of suspicion between the two sides. Hatred, tension, and uncertainties that develop are what make these wars so brutal and both sides so reluctant to make concessions that could bring them to agreement. The intractability of the Israeli-Palestinian story exemplifies this.

The difficulty in negotiating an end comes from lack of security. Neither side can make commitments to peace, to stop fighting, to demobilize troops. If rebels disarm first, they become vulnerable to the very forces that have been trying to defeat them. The government, then, has the incentive and the ability to wipe out their remaining forces. Armed wings of political movements must disassemble, and rebel leaders are understandably reluctant to face the unpredictability of elections. This impasse makes for a critical role for the rest of the world. Many political leaders do choose to settle their conflict even when they have to make compromises to do so, and if there are not enough incentives to negotiate an end from within, they must be provided from outside. The difficulty revolves around just how to do this right. Getting it right is the stuff of international politics and interventions into the affairs of other countries.

Although relevant, questions of international morality and law fall by the wayside when notions of national interest are brought to the forefront: In the world of international politics governments intervene when it is in their interest to do so. For example, the U.S. invasions of Iraq and Afghanistan could be thought of in terms of interventions into civil wars. The objective in these cases was not to foster negotiated outcomes. It was military defeat. In spite of the legal or normative implications of U.S. policy toward Iraq or Afghanistan, the United States was going to do what it was going to do. And the U.S. is not going to intervene to defeat the Palestinians or the Israelis, or try to overthrow the Kabila regime in the Congo in order to stop the civil war there. It is best to focus on pragmatic rather than normative and legal aspects of how to solve civil wars.

Countries intervene quite regularly to try to stop or manage civil wars in other countries, sometimes with great fanfare, as the United States did in Somalia in 1990 or in Bosnia in 1994. The more prominent U.S. interventions in recent years include embargoing funds to the Palestinians, particularly Hamas; the military intervention to oust the Taliban in Afghanistan; and the diplomatic efforts to end the Bosnian civil war. And one of the more divisive interventions was in support of the Contras in Nicaragua during the 1980s. I experienced that one firsthand.

The firefight that woke me that morning in Quilali was between Contra rebels, using automatic weapons supplied by the Americans, and the Sandinista, returning fire with their Soviet-supplied weapons. The two countries were involved in the civil war of a third, and together they made the war more protracted and bloody than it would have been. Their support was enough to ensure a military stalemate, and the political demands of either side were nothing short of dissolution of the opponent. The war continued because political compromise was unacceptable, but also because military victory, thanks to the intervention, was unachievable.

Conventional wisdom suggests that these interventions during the Cold War were proxy wars between the United States and the Soviet Union. From this vantage point each side claimed the ideological high ground, as did their patron. There can be little doubt that the Cold War played out in part through interventions in civil wars, but by my count there were only a handful of instances where the United States and the USSR directly intervened on opposing sides in the same civil war. These very visible interventions by the two superpowers might have distorted the impression of the role of interventions as a tool for the strong to muck in the affairs of the weak.

Interventions cannot be designed to make wars bloodier or longer, or to prevent settlement. The immediate goal of most interventions is to end the fighting, or keep it stopped if it has already ended. These intentions may sometimes be violated at the margins and it may seem as though intentions and goals of intervening parties are not always altruistic. But even from a purely practical standpoint, trying to influence the outcome of a civil war is a complicated and costly undertaking. It could be arming a rebel outfit, bolstering the military of a government at war, giving economic aid, providing diplomatic support and encouragement, or even imposing sanctions. Each of these actions requires the use of national treasure, political prestige, or both. If troops are involved, there is a risk of shedding national blood. No country, therefore, gets involved in the civil war of another without good reason. Most of the time that reason involves humanitarian concerns or national interest. Humanitarian issues seemed to be at the core of President Bush's decision to intervene in Somalia in 1992, and national interests were clearly driving the other President Bush to intervene in Afghanistan in 2001. Neither of these two broad goals would be advanced by prolonging a civil war.

A government intervening to support a rebel group would naturally want them to win, but a quick victory would be preferable to a long war. Even the intervener's goal of winning is sometimes in doubt. The United States, for example, always proclaimed that its support for the Contra army in Nicaragua was not designed to overthrow the Nicaraguan government, but rather to force the government to negotiate with the rebels. If that was the case, the strategy probably worked.

The U.S. intervention in Nicaragua has been described as both starting the civil war and helping to end it. Could both be right? It is not technically fair to say that the United States started the Contra movement seeking to overthrow the Sandinistas in Nicaragua. What is more accurate is that a budding band of ex-Somoza soldiers were looking for a way to support their struggle against the new Nicaraguan government. At first they were poor, underequipped, and in desperate condition. But they were just the band of insurgents that the Reagan administration was looking for. With a lot of help from the United States the Contras grew into a large and well-equipped fighting force. Intervention by the U.S., from this perspective, made a civil war where there might not otherwise have been one. Much later it was the congressional cutoff of aid to the Contras that shaped the expectations of their fortunes on the battlefield. Without U.S. military support the Contras could never have hoped to defeat the Sandinista government. The calculations of the rebels were influenced by outside interventions. A concerted diplomatic effort to reach a solution turned the changing situation on the battlefields into an opportunity to reach a negotiated settlement. It might be fair to say that without the U.S. infusion of guns there would have been no Contra army, but it is also fair to say that the effect of cutting off aid under a congressional mandate influenced prospects for a negotiated solution. The Contra army compelled concessions from the Sandinista government that they otherwise would not have made.

The Guatemalan civil war lasted nearly thirty years and killed one hundred fifty thousand people; fifty thousand civilians "disappeared" at the hands of government forces. When I was there the fear was palpable, and any faith in so repressive a government was at best questionable. I got the sense that people wanted peace and normalcy in their lives, even though they were unhappy at conditions that led to the war and unhappy with their government's response. The United States gave training, helicopters, and money to the government, but other outside interventions were primarily diplomatic, in the form of mediators. Military support to the rebels at the later stages could have helped create the environment for a settlement. That never happened. By the time an agreement was reached the rebels were no longer strong enough militarily to make much of a demand on the government. They fought for a generation, suffered horribly, and got very little for their efforts. Had they been a more capable fighting force there might have been more incentive for the government to negotiate, and they might have forced a better deal in the process. I faced many questions about what "my" government was doing and why, and I often wondered what the United States could do differently if its first priority was peace. The war ended nearly a decade after I left, so the question still remains as to whether the U.S. could have helped orchestrate the same peaceful outcome much earlier. Could a different policy of intervention have eliminated ten years of war, torture, disappearances, and killing? Was it the motives and preferences of the rebels and the Guatemalan government or the motives and interests of the United States that prevented a negotiated agreement much earlier?

There are two roles that outsiders can play in managing civil wars: One is, of course, to stop the fighting. The other is to keep it stopped and work toward peace. Stopping the fighting is a long way from an agreement that will put a conflict to rest. But it is the first step before trust, confidence, and the country itself can be rebuilt. If those fighting a civil war bring it to an end but do not address conditions that led to war in the first place, there is a very real chance of a return to war. One civil war takes generations to get over, but a series of wars that result from unresolved issues prevents a country from developing a political, social, and economic infrastructure. People in countries that have undergone such wars continually suffer from poverty, discrimination, helplessness, hopelessness, physical abuse, and early death.

The tools used to influence civil wars fall into the three sweeping categories of military, economic, and diplomatic strategies. These tools describe the different options available to a government, the UN, or an international organization trying to influence the outcome of a civil war. Each of these agencies has a limited set of options at its disposal, options that are consistent with its mission. A military, for example, would transfer guns, give military intelligence, fly sorties—actions consistent with the tools available to them. And while a Department of State or a Ministry of Foreign Affairs has no military aid to give, it has diplomatic skills and resources to bring to the negotiating table in pursuit of a peaceful resolution.

Military interventions are most visible, most threatening, most contentious, and most likely to embroil a country in someone else's civil war. At some point this is the story of Vietnam, El Salvador, Nicaragua, and Iraq. One of the more common forms of military intervention is supplying guns and ammunition to either a rebel group or the government. Tanks, jeeps, helicopters, guns, ammo, and communication equipment would all be on the list of military goods requested and delivered. Anything, in fact, that makes it more likely for one side to have a better chance of winning.

The more violent the war, obviously, the faster both sides will run out of weapons and ammunition. During the Soviet invasion of Afghanistan and the long war that ensued, the United States supported the opposition rebel movement. Millions and millions of rounds of ammunition were needed to keep the Afghanis in the field fighting the Soviets, and this immense quantity of bullets and military supplies kept the U.S. working hard to meet the demand. Military interventions can also include weapons that are much more lethal and sophisticated than bullets and rifles. The U.S. gave the Afghani mujahideen Stinger missiles. At the time these were cutting-edge, shoulder-fired, heat-seeking antiaircraft missiles, and they were famously effective at neutralizing the Soviets' superior technology in the air.

It would be reasonable to conclude that a military intervention—supplying the means of warfare to either side—is at odds with my assertion that interventions are intended to stop the fighting. Although it is easy to accept the idea that helping with the negotiating process is good for prospects of peace, it is much harder to accept that military support to either side can advance the peace process. Sometimes it does.

Military victory for one side and military defeat for the other is one way—the most common way—for civil wars to end. Usually, the government wins. If the goal is to end a war, helping one side militarily defeat its enemy might sometimes be effective. An abundance of weapons, advanced technology, military intelligence, advisors, and troops in combat can all turn the tide of battle in favor of one side or the other. Che Guevara, an icon of revolutionary movements the world over, was pursued relentlessly in the mountains of Bolivia with the help of U.S. military and intelligence units. He was hunted down and captured, bedraggled and malnourished, nothing like the image portrayed today. Within a day, and with the approval of the United States, he was executed. He did not have much of a chance to organize an effective rebel force. From a different perspective, with U.S. help, the Bolivians were able to end his rebellion quickly, though his mythology lives on.

Civil wars can also end through negotiations that determine the future relationship between the government and the rebels. Agreeing to a settlement is really a matter of managing a negotiated outcome in light of expectations for victory. If you were a rebel leader or soldier, you would already have made some demands on the government, which would either have taken those demands seriously, or not. Part of what determines how seriously it has taken these demands is how capable you are of pressing for them on the battlefield. Like the rebels in Guatemala who fought for twenty years, if your band of rebels has been unable to disrupt much of the country, and you were unable to convince a lot of young people to join your cause, the government will be unwilling to concede very much. If rebels who are considerably weaker than the government opt to negotiate before they are militarily defeated, they will be forced to make most of the concessions. When there is some chance the rebels could actually beat the government, the government might be better off finding a way out that leaves them some role in governing the country. This is the critical difference between the uprising I wandered into in Bangladesh, which was repressed in a matter of days, and the civil wars in Guatemala and Nicaragua. In the two Central American countries the rebels were able to press their demands by force of arms. As the two wars dragged on, the ability of the Guatemalan rebels waned while that of the Nicaraguan Contras increased. The Contras received a lot of U.S. support while the Guatemalan rebels ran out of options. It seemed quite clear neither government was going to win on the battlefield, so it was only a matter of time before the two sides figured out how to negotiate an acceptable outcome. In Guatemala this took a generation.

For an individual rebel soldier trying to figure out whether or not to stay with her band of brothers, the relative power of the government may be a determining factor. If prospects for victory look dim, then defection may be the option. The amount of outside military hardware and support the rebels expect to get also influences this decision. One of the frustrations of the budding Contra army in Nicaragua was that military support initially came far too slowly to keep the rebel recruits armed and fed. As frustration mounted they began to walk away from the rebel army. As the military balance changes, so too do prospects for making political concessions. President Ronald Reagan came to the rescue of the beleaguered Contras, and rather than a crushing defeat, they ended up with a negotiated outcome that resulted in power sharing with the Sandinistas.

In general, you don't win a war unless you have the military capability to do so. And although it is not a hard and fast rule, those with the bigger and better military are more likely to win the war. Outside military interventions tend to influence this balance of power. Military capabilities influence decisions about when to fight, when to make demands, when to negotiate, and when to make concessions. Expectations that result from each side's understanding of the military balance are critical. Both sides might hold unreasonable expectations by estimating the forces of the enemy incorrectly, or by overestimating their own support in the local community, but it is expectations for victory or defeat that influence decisions, right or wrong. These are also the factors that can be manipulated by military interventions.

When weapons, intelligence, or troops are delivered to one side in a civil war, that side is emboldened and is more likely to think that they have a better chance of winning on the battlefield. They might also calculate that with another country on their side they have improved their chance of winning and reduced their need to make concessions, or even negotiate. If the government gets outside help, its leadership will probably conclude it now has the capability to put down the rebellion, and only if necessary settle the conflict short of victory. And given the new dynamics of military capabilities, it might expect to get much more if negotiations do take place. One of the things we think we know about the bargaining that takes place in the midst of wars is that the relative power of the two parties influences the bargaining positions that they will take. In short, all people or groups are not equal when it comes to negotiating the end to a war. Basically, the stronger you are, the less you have to concede, and if you are weak relative to your enemy, you might be better off taking a bad agreement than being beaten and thoroughly defeated. In that case you would get next to nothing. It should come as no surprise, then, that a military intervention can play an awfully big role in determining this balance of power.

Logic would suggest that military interventions will help the weaker side more than the stronger—the more an intervention accounts for the total amount of military capabilities, the more important it is to that group. In most cases the rebels start off much weaker than the government. Think about a small rebel group with only enough weapons and ammunition to fight for a short period. If a country like the United States sent them military aid, the aid could double or triple their stock of weapons, as with the Contras. But if the United States sent the exact same amount of aid to a government, it might represent only a small drop in the otherwise big bucket of military capability.

In the recent history of Afghanistan was a decade-long, horrific civil war, and during the latter part of the 1990s the Taliban started to win. By 2001 they controlled most of the country, though an opposition force, the Northern Alliance, was holding out against them. When the United States intervened to oust the Taliban, it didn't send in a large army designed to defeat a national opponent as it did in Iraq. It sent a lot of military support for the Northern Alliance. The U.S. support for the Northern Alliance turned the tide in the civil war and the Alliance quickly defeated the government forces. It did win, but as we know today, the war is not over. The basic problems confronting that country were not resolved, even though the balance of power shifted quite dramatically in favor of the Northern Alliance.

There is also the difficulty that if one country supports one side in a civil war, some other country might support the other side. The evidence suggests that you get what you pay for in this type of situation: bigger, longer, bloodier wars. Nothing really changes in the calculation about whether or not, and when, it is a good time to make some concessions. This would probably be true for the foot soldier and the leader alike. A soldier who might just have received a new rifle and new boots, maybe even a jeep, now feels ready to go, a soldier in an army that can win. This is not the normal tool for managing conflicts, but it is certainly the image of U.S. and Soviet interventions during the Cold War. And as we saw during that period, few of them ended until the Cold War did.

To my mind, it doesn't matter that much what form a military intervention takes. If a country sends in intelligence, guns and ammunition, troops, or close air support for operations, it is going to ratchet up rather than ratchet down the conflict unless the intervention is clearly designed to facilitate a quick victory. There are exceptions to this general conclusion, but they are not common. The United States in Afghanistan is an instance where the level of the intervention was massive. The U.S. effort was in fact so large that the intervention overwhelmed the Afghani army. Another exception is Rwanda in 1994.

The French intervened with military troops at the end of the most brutal period, and that was enough to put a halt to the fighting. By this point the slaughter had reached fever pitch, and the tide seemed to be turning in favor of the Tutsis, so the French role was simply to provide a way out. In general, military interventions influence the fighting capabilities of each side, but this tends to make continued fighting more, not less, likely.

Although it is not a perfect analogy, the United States is mired in Iraq today in part because U.S. policy emphasized the military aspects of the intervention over political or economic ones. Had economic incentives and diplomacy taken precedence over the coercive capability of the U.S. military, 2007 might not have been the deadliest year of the war. The United States simply didn't put in place the conditions under which negotiations and concessions were possible.

Outside interventions are attempts to influence the ability of a government or rebels to press their demands on the battlefield and make them stick at the negotiating table, and money can be as influential as guns if given in the right way. Economic support changes the way insurgent groups or governments can operate. From an insurgent's point of view money can be used to buy food, pay recruits, or pay off local communities. Economic aid allows a government to transfer money from a multitude of other programs into the fight against the insurgents. In either case economic support can have an effect on the willingness to fight or negotiate, just as military support can. The economic squeeze on the Palestinians after the election of Hamas seriously constrained average Palestinian families. Work was hard to come by, tourism dried up, and individuals had to consider the cost of resistance to the occupation. The armed men I met with in the refugee camp in the West Bank seemed to have responded with greater resolve to fight, but some people I met saw capitulation as the best strategy to end the economic embargo. In using its economic leverage the United States supported Israel's effort to suppress opposition recruitment. As a tool of intervention the embargo may turn out to be remarkably effective at breaking the back of the Palestinian resistance, at least in the short term.

Economic aid can take many forms when used as a tool to influence the outcome of civil wars. It can be used to support those fighting or as enticement for both sides to quit. We most often think of grants and loans, but there are all sorts of monetary credits that can be given. During November 2004, there was talk of forgiving Iraq's massive foreign debt. To banks and countries that were owed, it was not a great deal of money—billions of dollars distributed across a long list of countries—but to the fledgling Iraqi government it could have made a substantial difference. There are also economic sanctions that can be used to influence the behavior of the parties to the conflict, as with the Palestinians. Withdrawing aid, imposing restrictions on a country's ability to borrow money, or cutting off channels for trade can be vitally constraining to a government leader trying to raise money to fight a civil war or find resources with which to make concessions. This is one of the frontline strategies in the fight against Al Qaeda and its bases of operation. The U.S. and other countries have tied up their bank accounts, social service agencies, and other sources of funds.

There are a host of sources for economic support, including governments, the United Nations, the International Monetary Fund, the World Bank, and regional organizations. The link between economic interventions and the attempt to influence a civil war is less transparent than that of military interventions. Guns are primarily tools to advance killing. Money can be used to support the war, but it can also be used to relieve hardship, prevent starvation, and advance the economy. Depending on the timing of the use of economic assistance, it can have an effect on the ability to wage war or the terms of a peace agreement. There are also private voluntary organizations that can weigh in with a more meager range of resources. CARE, World Vision, and Oxfam can all contribute, even if not in the same league as governments or the UN.

Economic leverage has the potential to go a long way to getting those fighting a civil war to rethink their approach. Economics, after all, is right at the foundation of civil wars—economic conditions that are driven by bad politics, but economic problems nonetheless. The government of a country that has bankrupted itself fighting an insurgency may be unable to find the resources to accede to the demands of its opposition even if it wanted to do so. Economic aid may alter the situation enough to get both sides to lay down arms. The evidence we have, though, is at best mixed. Like military support, this, too, is a double-edged sword. Money can be turned into weapons, supporting the war rather than a peace effort. The problem is not so much in the type of intervention but rather in how the intervention is carried out. Haphazard, incoherent, poorly motivated, or uncoordinated efforts to influence a civil war send all the wrong signals and end up creating more havoc than progress toward peace.

We can start with the premise that good intentions will not be enough because rebel soldiers or governments fighting for their survival will care a lot less about good intentions than they will about the practical—terms of a settlement or military capability. To be effective the money must be used to generate concessions, to make it easier to stop fighting than to keep fighting. Far too many times, outside governments and international organizations ship in money, attach a few strings related to how the recipient should spend it, and hope these cash-infused economic reforms will work. They don't. To get into a civil war the government most likely engaged in a fair bit of brutal repression of the opposition before the opposition actually took up arms. Money is unlikely to immediately solve these problems without attention to some of the other issues that drove the rebels to take the risks associated with warfare.

Any intervener must also consider the risk that rebels, or the government that receives the cash, will not use it to make peace, strings or no strings. Why would they not, for instance, just use it to help their side win the war, or to further enrich the leaders? The first instincts of a rebel leader or president of a country might not be land reform, subsidies, or jobs. They might instead choose to turn the cash into weapons on the market or buy loyalty from political cronies. Former president Mobutu of Zaire did just that. He took billions of dollars in grants, squirreled it away in Swiss banks, and paid it out to his political supporters. By the late 1990s he was defeated by his opponents. But in the interim, for all the aid he received, he only made the economic conditions in his country worse.

Part of the problem is that there is not enough money or capital investments to pull the economy out of the ravages of a war. Any peace arrangement requires the disarmament of a lot of soldiers, and from their point of view, giving up their jobs as soldiers. During the war it might well have been the only form of income that they had, so giving it up without any hope for a better job would not go over very well. In a bankrupt economy there is no immediate way to create new jobs, and for an intervention to be effective the initial conditions that led to the uprising have to be addressed.

A key in using economic interventions as productive "carrots" is to design them in a way that will build confidence in the most critical participants of the war. Most of the research would suggest that these are rebel soldiers, rebel leaders, and political and economic elites who have been supporting the government. You have to go back to the conditions at the start of the war, and compare them with conditions that are evident at the time the war has the potential to end. What is missing? An effective institutional infrastructure is one thing that will need rebuilding, and economic assistance can surely help here. What are the important institutions and just what do they do?

Think about all the basic institutions of government that you will run into in any given day, and what would happen if any one or all of them were nonexistent, nonfunctional, or reserved exclusively for the wealthy. On a given day, you will probably drive down a road that will have traffic lights, police officers, and crossing guards. If you work you'll pay taxes. Power is supplied to your house. If you are a farmer, you live and die by the way your country regulates and subsidizes the agricultural industry. When you travel by plane or train, there is an institution that regulates, inspects, and controls the infrastructure to get you where you are going. And when you watch TV or listen to the radio, the airwaves are regulated. If you live at the lower boundaries of the socioeconomic ladder, there are institutions that help with housing, food, medical access, and support of children. Schools and hospitals: where they are located, who can go to them, and which community gets new ones are important components that would be of concern to you. These are all part of the critical institutional infrastructure that may have been underdeveloped before the war started, and decrepit, depleted, even destroyed as the war approaches its end point. These are also institutions that will help to keep the country from fracturing again, keep the farmer in the fields and out of a rebel camp, the worker employed and not carrying a gun—institutions that will help remove motivations for those at the margins to rise up against the government. When these institutions are destroyed the odds of fighting another civil war are high. External financial assistance might be critical for forging the peace. But just giving money is not enough to convince both sides that the time has come to settle the conflict.

Think about it this way: if you can't demobilize the soldiers you cannot get peace. You can't demobilize soldiers if they have nothing to go back to. People must have jobs; people must have some reason to expect that life after the end of the war will be better than at the beginning of it. Rebel soldiers will not lay down their weapons without some expectation that promises can and will be fulfilled. I have often wondered what it would have taken to keep the men in Quilali, Nicaragua, at home instead of out in the hills with the Contra rebels. There did not appear to be a great ideological rift between the people of the town and the Sandinista soldiers who were staying there. The payoff for participating with the Contras was high, literally. They were hired with U.S. funds. To intervene effectively you would have to deal with the grievances, address the economic value of participation, and be able to manage the risk. That is, to make it financially possible for the individual to quit the war, and make it safe for him or her to do so without fear of recrimination by either rebels or government troops. That is a tall task. To do this you have to have a government that can function efficiently and effectively, and for this task money is important. But to make economic aid an effective tool for managing a civil war, it has got to be tied to the ending of hostilities.

Military or economic interventions by themselves don't work because they just aren't designed for the task at hand. It seems almost naive to think that giving money or guns to one side in a civil war could be an effective way to get them to think about settlement. It is putting too much responsibility on a tool that is not capable of achieving the desired goals. Part of what is missing is the context under which this type of support is given. If you think about the message that is sent along with the money or guns, you will see why. If a shipment of guns is given with the message that "we support your cause," the message—implicit or explicit—is to fight on. What is the cause of the rebels at that time? To defeat the government.

An alternative message, one that emphasizes concessions and negotiations, can have a different impact. Imagine a message that conveyed, "Here is enough support to compel significant concessions from the rebels; now start negotiating." It is quite a different form of intervention than the first one. In the latter instance there is a clear link to diplomacy around which a settlement can be crafted. The military or economic support might still be important, even instrumental, but without the message of negotiation it might fuel the flames of war rather than dampen them.

There were 153 civil wars between 1945 and 1999. Sixty-eight of them had outside mediators trying to help bring the sides to an agreement; the other eighty-five did not. And those wars in which mediators got involved usually had a number of independent attempts to reach settlement. Ending ongoing civil wars requires considerably more than just the carrot, just the stick, or even the carrot and the stick. Many will end on their own through victory and defeat. It is the ones that don't, often the longest and most deadly, that require outside help, and the evidence shows that mediation is a factor in shortening civil wars. The most effective route to using the resources of a third country to bring an end to a civil war is to combine carrots and sticks through the use of diplomacy.

Quite often these civil wars are in countries you are unfamiliar with, on continents you may never have traveled to. But if we have learned anything in the past seven years, it is that these remote civil wars can have grave consequences for regional and global stability. The events of September 11, 2001, were possible in part because of an unresolved civil war in Afghanistan. And the war of choice in Iraq was the culmination of nearly three decades of civil war in that country. Sudan, Somalia, Cambodia, and Rwanda are all grim reminders that none of us, if we consider ourselves part of the world community, are immune from the horrific consequences that result when communities of people rise up against their own.

12

♦ ♦ ♦

PERSUASION

The breakup of the former Yugoslavia and the civil war in Bosnia generated a trail of carnage visible to all the world. This conflict created a conundrum for Western leaders. This was, it must be remembered, the region from which the First World War spawned. Each side in the conflict had its traditional allies in a world uncertain enough that the smallest mistakes held the seeds of a larger disaster. Any intervention, although critical to peace and stability, called for delicacy and caution.

There are many ways to help end civil wars short of victory for one side. The Dayton Peace Accords, which served as the foundation for ending the Bosnian war in 1995, are a prominent example of what can be done. But it took numerous efforts by former U.S. secretary of state Cyrus Vance and former British foreign secretary Lord Owen before they were able to broker a deal. The U.S. government invested its political clout to forge an agreement that moved all sides from the front lines to an uneasy peace deal. Just the agreement wasn't enough. It took commitment by the global community to stay involved, help rebuild war-torn communities, and ensure compliance with terms of the agreement. The key part of that effort was political intervention by the United States. This same type of high-level political investment and mediation was instrumental in bringing the conflict in Northern Ireland to an end in 1999. On the other hand, most governments have shied away from any resolute action in Darfur, Sudan, although the horrors of that civil war have created a humanitarian crisis that rivals Bosnia. My sense is that there are two reasons operating simultaneously for the difference in response. The reason for action in Bosnia and Northern Ireland is that these are European countries, and the West has a preference for stability among people of a common culture. The reasons for inaction in Africa involve lack of a coherent strategy—not knowing what works and when—and the lack of a similar commitment to Africa.

Since 1945 there have been over 150 civil wars, some long ones, some short. And between 1945 and 2000 there have been over a thousand individual military or economic interventions by outside governments or other political organizations. Most of these interventions involved military support for one side in the conflict. These interventions, despite the best intentions, fail to help stop the fighting in most cases, and on average they led to longer, not shorter, civil wars. Almost every study concludes that military intervention fuels the fires of civil wars rather than bringing them under control. It is premature, though, to dismiss all interventions as counterproductive based on this evidence. It would be premature even to dismiss all military interventions without considering the outcomes when they are used in conjunction with the other options available. Carrots and sticks, the common approach to intervention, tend to leave out mediation. The U.S. effort to end the Bosnian war was one instance where all three were used quite adroitly.

Logic and early evidence do point to a different outcome if a combination of mediation and weapons or money was used to send the right message. The ability to use force makes negotiations more effective in helping implacable foes find a way out of their troubles. The main question is whether mediation trumps all other efforts to bring civil wars to an end.

To understand how mediation might act as the levee between peace and war, we have to go back to what is happening on the battlefields and in the command headquarters. The willingness of each side to sign a peace deal is related to two important things: their expectations for victory on the battlefield, and what they expect to gain from victory or a settlement. The strong will push for greater concessions and the weak might sue for peace if they believe they face defeat. Understanding these expectations is absolutely critical to achieving an agreement. Most descriptions of the end of the civil war in El Salvador (1992), for instance, show that the government was holding back on signing an agreement because it thought it could get more out of the rebels. It changed its bargaining strategy only after the rebels engaged in one last—and quite effective—offensive. The rebels took over much of the capital city, San Salvador, and demonstrated that they could not be defeated. But since the offensive didn't force the government to collapse, it also demonstrated that the rebels could not win outright. A military stalemate seemed secure. It was only after this point that the government began to move toward a more cooperative position, and a peace agreement was reached shortly thereafter.

Not all rebel groups can pull off an offensive as a tool to force concessions from a government as neatly as that, and not all governments can be assured that such an offensive is not possible. The expectations of both sides are born of estimates of their own and their opponents' military capability and political resolve. But these estimates are sometimes wrong. Either side can overinflate their own capabilities and the likelihood of victory, and then refuse to negotiate because they think that they can win, just as either side can underestimate the chances of their opponent winning. In the early stages of negotiations neither side in the war has an incentive to give a complete picture of what they foresee happening on the battlefield. Imagine a rebel commander coming into the negotiations admitting that he has very low expectations of victory, that his forces are nearly out of ammunition, and that morale is dismally low. The government would then be smart to walk away from the negotiating table and start an offensive to finish off the rebels. So the rebels have to deceive the government, and the government, likewise, tries to deceive the rebels. Complete information from within, then, is elusive. An outside mediator can help change this dynamic, and in the process move the sides closer to an agreement. For a mediator, information—objective information about the "real" military balance—is the key to securing concessions that can lead to a peace agreement.

In my small community I serve as a public mediator. The intuition I gain from this role contributes to my thinking about the role of diplomacy. A public mediator really plays a low-level role in helping members of the community resolve their seemingly simple problems before they end up in court. The issues are rarely life and death; they are about locks, dogs, and cars. The principal tasks, however, are amazingly similar to mediation in civil wars. These minor squabbles I deal with are between friends or family members unable to come to terms with the problem at hand, totally disrupting relationships with stunning regularity. Lovers fight, neighbors don't speak to each other, and uncles and nieces become estranged, mostly over difficulty in confronting emotional aspects of their problems. Rarely does success or failure of mediation turn completely on the cost of the lock or full reimbursement for a faulty repair. Communication, information, and emotions at times outweigh the importance of the underlying issue. As a mediator I know it is almost impossible to get people to the point of an agreement unless you can get them to recognize the hurt, the pain, and the emotional costs. Certainly the issues within a civil war are not like a changed lock or a murderous dog, but many of the same types of costs are at the foundation of a civil war. They must be. A peasant farmer, a factory worker, or a child, given a gun and asked to kill members of his own country, is not likely to do so without being swept up in the emotion of the situation. But it is not only the psychology of a conflict that makes resolution difficult. These are people who have taken huge risks for a goal, and do not give up on these goals very easily. This is particularly true of the leadership of the rebels and the government. There is a lot more at stake than the issues that started them down the road to civil war. Expectations can also change with information. Emotional commitment, security risks, costs of failure—all influence the estimation of an adversary's capabilities and the chances of victory. Misleading the opponent, if not self-deception, would be the norm between two sides fighting a civil war. This plays out even in the small-time mediations over car repairs, changed locks, or the dissolution of a marriage.

When we think about managing civil wars, most people think of diplomacy. The role of military or economic interventions is less intuitive than trying to use the skills of a diplomat to achieve a negotiated outcome. It would surprise few of us to know that, even though mediators got involved in only about 40 percent of the civil wars in the last half of the twentieth century, and there were military interventions in over 60 percent of them, most of the evidence points to mediation being much more effective than military efforts at shortening a civil war. It is, actually, hard to help your side win a war, and considerably easier to help them negotiate an acceptable set of political arrangements to end it. Using diplomacy is the more effective approach to ending civil wars, even though it is less often used.

One of the problems associated with ending civil wars—most wars, for that matter—is that it is difficult to get people who have been fighting to make concessions necessary to narrow the distance between their bargaining positions. Giving a little bit might make you appear weak, and in the midst of fighting a war, that is the last thing you want. Neither side wants to make the first concession. In my experiences with community mediation I find that I am sometimes able to coax it out of a person in private. But when the parties are brought in together, that small concession becomes much more elusive; it is rarely a willing embrace in public. The fear of appearing too willing to make concessions pulls people back. Making concessions is revealing weakness, vulnerability, and a readiness to give up the fight. In war, weakness is fatal. In war, the ability to press your opponent is tied to the relative military prowess of each side: revealing weakness has the potential of emboldening the enemy. An outside mediator can lighten the load on the parties in the war.

What works in small community environments also works in the bigger issues of war and peace. Mediation is a form of conflict management in which an outside party to the conflict sends in someone to help the two sides figure out how to get out of their mess. A mediator's role can range from acting as the person who passes along information to offering solutions or arranging the resources required to implement an agreement. Sometimes the mediator has the simple but important task of bringing the warring parties into the same room. This is a crucial first step and is actually the point at which each side recognizes that conditions do exist that could lead to a negotiated settlement. Each side basically accepts the notion of making concessions when they agree to negotiate, and just having an outside person present while they discuss the issues that are keeping them at war can help. A mediator can also play a quite forceful role, providing money, security, technical assistance. It is in this stronger role that a mediator can make suggestions that neither side could dare venture to make. Sometimes it is the stature of the person that is important, sometimes it is the depth of the pockets of the country sending the mediator. Sometimes both are important. President Jimmy Carter has made a distinguished career out of his role as a mediator. He brings his moral stature to the table, even though he does not really bring resources. This man is known around the world as a champion of human rights, and people feel confident that he will use his personal stature to stand by them. An official representative of the U.S. government can come to the table with the authority to contribute materially as well as politically in ways that help make peace possible. In the Egyptian-Israeli negotiations, those between the Palestinians and Israelis, as well as the Dayton Accords, the U.S. government used its authority to push the players toward an agreement, and it also committed billions of dollars in cash to help sweeten any deal.

It is shortsighted, though, to think that the infusion of money, arms, loans, or credits alone will get the central players to move toward a peaceful outcome. Most of these types of aid are so wound up in political processes that they are clumsy as tools of conflict management, at least as an independent method of trying to bring peace. Diplomatic efforts, on the other hand, are specifically targeted at developing negotiating positions. It would seem, intuitively at least, that diplomatic channels would at least provide some mechanism to get those fighting to move closer to an agreement, and that an agreement could come out of sending a peace delegation. Most of the evidence, however, points out that much of the time, diplomatic efforts to end a civil war—or any war—fail to hammer out an agreement.

Getting two sides to agree to quit fighting is not easy, and it certainly should not be a surprise that any one mediation attempt is unlikely to be successful. One side might feel that the timing is right to negotiate an agreement, but so too must its enemy. It takes two to fight, and so two to negotiate. When two sides fighting a war agree to sit down together, there is an implicit understanding that an agreement is possible, or even preferable. Still, peace remains elusive, and the early negotiations usually fail. But just the acknowledgment that settlement is preferred over continued warfare is a big first step. The history of peace agreements, stalled peace processes, Qassam rockets, and Israeli air strikes are testament to the difficulty of making peace in spite of highly placed and determined mediators.

Recognizing potential for a negotiated end to fighting comes with recognition that victory may not be achievable at the time. At this point at least some concessions are possible. We also have to keep in mind that at the early stage of the negotiations neither side is openly confronting the "true" arrangement of military capabilities. Each side may prefer a negotiated route, but neither will reveal their true status and suffer the fatal blow of appearing weak. A negotiated settlement might be acceptable if the terms were favorable, if each side got most of what they wanted. But war might still be preferred to granting too many concessions. Without an outside mediator the two sides can easily get locked into a cycle that is driven by the need to avoid appearing weak. The leaders have to recognize that they are going to have to make choices about what they value most and what they are willing to fight for. Some things might be worth dying for, some are not. That remains very private information.

In early 2008 the Israelis and Palestinians were going through this jockeying process. Palestinians in Gaza shot rockets into Israel, then Israel demonstrated its superior capabilities by sending troops back into Gaza. In the West Bank the Palestinian president called for calm, all the while equivocating about whether or not to keep negotiations open. All this was taking place while the U.S. secretary of state was in the country to act as a mediator. Little by way of substantive issues seemed to be addressed. As the violence continued and shaky efforts to negotiate sputtered and squeaked, I often thought about the three resistance fighters who took the considerable risk to meet with me. I wonder if they are now casualties of the renewed fighting, or in prison, or dead. Negotiating an end to the conflict that might extract them from their conditions looks so very difficult even when the solution is largely in sight.

There are two things that a mediator can do at this juncture. One is to get both sides to reveal only to the mediator some of that private information. Then, the mediator can use it to shape possible ways out of an impasse. Neither rebels nor government would appear weak because they would not be the ones suggesting the concessions. A mediator can allow each side to articulate the sources of their grievances, to describe their view of costs of war and the tactics that have been used against them, and to engage in some of the social-psychological cleansing that can facilitate open negotiations. There will have been systematic discrimination, recriminations, human rights abuses, deceit, and excesses on both sides, all leading to mutual distrust, even hatred. This is the story of the Palestinian and Israeli impasse. They came close to a framework for an agreement in 1999, but clearly, close is not good enough. Though they continue to make halting progress, they are a long way from a peace agreement. The struggles in Northern Ireland went on for about thirty years; the Philippines have been fighting an insurgency for decades. Colombia seems unable to pull itself out of a twenty-year-long civil war. It may be that there is no way to divide the "pie," or that divisions are so extreme that solutions are not possible. When thinking about a positive outcome, however, it is more productive to focus on uncertainty and fears that surface as an agreement gets close rather than on the intractability of positions. Focusing on such concerns can make substantive concessions more acceptable. The mediator can make sure the types of issues that play out in the emotional arena are addressed.

If mediation has such great potential, why is it not used more often? There is little compelling evidence on this question, but the logic of mediation points to a rather straightforward answer. Mediation is voluntary. There is no such thing as mediation without one of the two groups at war. Both sides are needed at the table, so both sides have to recognize, and desire, a negotiated agreement. There must be some outcome in the range of possible agreements that both sides prefer to continued fighting. This is a restrictive set of conditions, particularly in the midst of a civil war. Until each side at least considers the possibility it might not win, negotiation holds little value. In a situation where rebels are too weak in the early stages of the war, they would not expect to get much at the negotiating table. They might decide to hold out until they can gather some forces and balance the military equation.

It is at this point, before negotiations begin, that both sides are potentially misperceiving, misestimating, and misrepresenting the relative military balance. If they think they can win, if they think a little more time will provide the victory, then they could avoid making those concessions. There are political costs to trying and failing, so if the time does not seem right, it might be best not to invest political capital.

What gets put on the negotiating table and what can the mediator bring? Everything is on the table, be it ethnic concerns, religious freedom or land rights, depending on each conflict. But a few things will be of primary importance. There were initial grievances that started the war, and at least some of those initial conditions will remain relevant throughout the war. Rebel leaders will have to give something to their soldiers. Land or economic reforms, union rights, political representation—all of these can work to overcome the inertia of the rebels to continue the fight. Security issues will be critical. Stopping fighting and surrendering weapons may pose greater risks to the rebels than their decision to take up arms in the first place. All the killing, destruction, and abuses from both sides will have bred distrust. Convincing the rebels or the government to demobilize their troops is not easy. A mechanism that allows this to happen in a way that leaves both sides reasonably secure will be important. And finally, the country will have to rebuild its political, social, and economic infrastructure. The government cannot agree to a settlement that does not provide the opportunity to rebuild. Stability is necessary for investments, institutions must be reestablished to deliver services and respond peacefully to the demands of the citizens, jobs need to be created for former soldiers. Each of these broad concerns will have to be part of the negotiation process.

The specific outcomes in these negotiations will be a function of many elements, including the balance of military power and the economic resources that are available in order to rebuild. This is where the mediator plays a crucial role. Sometimes the use of diplomacy can be combined with either arms or money to help compel or entice leaders to cut a deal. If the military balance is important, then adroit use of military aid or security assistance can be sufficient to push where diplomacy alone would be insufficient. One of the conclusions in a World Bank report on civil wars was that the sequencing of interventions was one of the best ways for outsiders to bring an end to a war. By "sequencing" I mean the ordering of intervention efforts: military first, then mediation, or vice versa. Sequencing provides an underlining strategy to an intervention, making it something that is not ad hoc, uninformed, or developed by some version of trial and error. A strategy conveys coherence.

In spite of the World Bank report's call for the adroit sequencing of interventions, we do not know much about what sequences work best or when. Our understanding of this process is meager because it is difficult to tease such information out of the data. This problem is being addressed; this line of inquiry represents the cutting edge of research into the effect of interventions. Logic, however, can guide our thinking about what makes sense as a good strategy. For instance, since the balance of military capabilities can translate into negotiating positions, military interventions that come just before rather than after attempts at mediation should provide a stronger foundation for peace. In fact, I think we can go as far as saying that the two should be linked, and linked in a particular order. Likewise, economics are so critical to the onset of civil war that using economic incentives to cement a peace agreement after negotiations should be more effective than giving the money before there are concessions at the bargaining table. Thinking about sequences is central to designing effective intervention strategies, and to my mind this begins to define the line between coherent strategies and ad hoc policy. Although any inference will have to remain vague until evidence can confirm this logic, the World Bank report makes considerable sense.

It is important to remember that we are trying to end a war, not get a better business deal or make good on a faulty car repair job. To get the sides to agree to the terms of a settlement they both have to prefer peace to war, expect that their opponents see things in a similar way, and trust the people they have been fighting to live up to the agreement. Imagine how hard this would be in Darfur, Sudan, or Sri Lanka, or Palestine and Israel. The men I met with in Palestine wanted peace just as much as any Israeli would, but getting to the point of trust and commitment and security will take a lot of effort. Moreover, the agreement has to result in a new set of conditions that both sides can agree to. In the terminology of the social sciences we say that mutual peace has to be a stable equilibrium. Peace can still break down into renewed warfare, but there also have to be conditions under which the peace agreement will hold. Those are the conditions that an outside intervention is trying to create. Just money usually doesn't get us there, nor will just more weapons.

The table illustrates the positions of those fighting a civil war, and how they must be induced to move their positions to achieve a peace agreement. I'm going to use this to describe the trick to intervening and why sequencing matters. In the figure there are four cells. The top right and bottom left cells, where one side prefers to fight and the other does not, reflect conditions of a civil war, even if both do not prefer this outcome. War happens because it is forced on one party by an opponent. All governments may claim this position before the initial outbreak of the civil war. But since at least one participant in the war would prefer to negotiate, there is some chance that interven-

Four Options Available to Those Fighting a Civil War

Both sides prefer peace negotiations and a peace agreement	The rebels prefer fighting; the government prefers negotiations
The government prefers fighting; the rebels prefer negotiations	Both sides prefer fighting

tions may motivate movement on the part of the other side. The other two cells are important because they are the two conditions that can become stable points—or equilibria. We can think of them as ideal points. In the bottom right cell the stable point is a war; in the top left it is a peace agreement. Moving the parties into the top left cell is the goal of interventions. Put differently, the goal is to make each side prefer to negotiate a settlement rather than fighting for their ideal outcome. This is where the skill of a mediator pays off. Signing an agreement does not mean that the two sides cannot or will not revert to war, but it is a first and necessary step.

The trick, if I can reiterate it, is to get the parties to consider a peace agreement a better outcome than continued fighting. If an intervening country weighs in by giving money or guns to one side while they are still in the frame of mind that keeps them in the trenches (bottom right), the probable outcome would be emboldened opponents. The key is to create movement toward the upper left cell of the table, and then use other resources to lock the parties into that position. Because willingness to negotiate is linked to expectations for victory, combining military aid with the power of diplomacy should help foster the necessary movement toward the conditions for peace. If the parties can be enticed up into the zone where an agreement is preferred, ensuring its terms are stable can be done by the infusion of economic incentives or by guaranteeing security. It is this type of mixing and sequencing that was highlighted by the World Bank report, and is what I believe lies at the heart of the most successful intervention strategies.

Emotions, fear, expectations, and customs can sometimes transcend the importance of the military balance or economic incentives. For a mediator, recognizing and using these less tangible aspects of a conflict to increase incentives for both sides can be vital. The material and structural aspects of the military standoff will remain important, but they might not be enough by themselves to move those making the decisions toward an agreement. It might seem hard to imagine that a peace agreement to end a civil war might hinge on things beyond power sharing, economic transfers, and the like, but they can and do.

When I think back to some of the community mediation that I have done, I can say that most of the movement toward a settlement comes after some recognition of the wrongs committed by each side. Once at that point, figuring out who owes whom and how much seems easy. The same elements can play out in civil wars. If you can get each side to accept that their opponent has a legitimate complaint, then you can use the resources available to help keep them focused on the steps needed to resolve the conflict

On January 9, 2005, the two sides in a twenty-one-year civil war signed a peace agreement. The war fought between those of northern and southern Sudan had all the hallmarks of group identity, economic exploitation, and psychology of war that make civil wars so complex and difficult. After several attempts, international mediators were able to pull together an acceptable agreement. The agreement spells out power-sharing and wealth-sharing arrangements, and all the technical details one would expect. Negotiations took two years to complete, and in the end neither side will demobilize its armed forces until all the terms of the agreement are fulfilled. They simply do not trust each other enough to go down that road yet. The peace talks were mediated by an organization of African states, while the United States, Norway, Great Britain, the European Union, Switzerland, and South Africa had all offered the prospects for economic and political assistance if the peace process holds. To some degree they may all just be looking to secure access to the oil reserves in that country, but a good strategy may hold the prospects for long-term peace in this troubled country. The agreement is a great start and brings with it the hope that the conflict in Darfur, Sudan, can also be resolved quickly. Getting the two sides to the Sudan conflict to agree to settle their differences required sensitivity to the consequences of twenty years of war, attention to the demands and complaints of the rebels, and the economic and diplomatic involvement of numerous outside actors. The first weeks of the negotiations involved just getting each side's story out on the table. By the end it was security guarantees, demobilization, distribution of resources, and economic incentives that were on the table. But to get to the substance they first had to deal with the traumas of war.

As successful as the negotiations in Sudan were, the conflict did last for two decades, leaving two million dead and many more refugees. Better intervention strategies may have been able to reduce the amount of time that the war raged. Though we are not there yet, the day is not far off when the research community will have a better handle on how best to sequence and time intervention techniques. Evidence does, however, point quite strongly to the important role of mediation. For example, a civil war with early diplomatic interventions can be expected to be shorter by up to 80 percent than those conflicts without mediation. When you consider that only 40 percent of the civil wars between 1945 and 1999 have had the involvement of outside mediators, there is plenty of room to improve the way the world responds to these internal political crises. The evidence is also beginning to point to the conclusion that the right combinations of interventions are much more successful than any one implement alone is.

When I mediate community disputes the end of the actual mediation meeting is the end of the process from my perspective. That is not so with civil wars. It takes a lot of dedication to keep things on track after the deal has been signed. How would you respond if you were the leader of a country that just signed a peace deal after years of civil war, and part of the deal required the demobilization of the rebel army? As soon as the rebels disarmed, would you go right back to war with a much superior army, and this time try to win quickly? If you know this, the rebels know it too, and are unlikely ever to disarm.

Getting a peace deal, then, and keeping the peace are two entirely different beasts.

13

◆ ◆ ◆

BLUE HELMETS AND
BLEU CHEESE

I n December 1991, Sir Brian Urquhart, former under-secretary general of the United Nations, wrote an article in the *New York Times* asking a question that is still tragically pertinent almost twenty years later: "Who can stop civil wars?"

In the article he pointed to one of the bigger problems in resolving civil wars: You need peace before you can put in peacekeepers, but without peacekeepers it is difficult to get peace. By the end of his argument, he focused on what is to me the more critical question. Is there something the United Nations can do, he asked, "or must the world continue to stand by and watch the carnage on television?" The implication is grim, but it is vitally important to analyze how the world should deal with civil wars. The questions he raised were never answered, at least not in any way that brings clarity and coherence to policy.

The political issues involved with putting together a UN force to intervene militarily in a civil war are difficult to overcome. Imagine your president or prime minister announcing on national television that she is going to send your soldiers to help stop someone else's war. Your troops would be commanded by another country's officers, their ability to fight back constrained, and in many instances it would not be clear whether they fight the host government or the rebels. Their assignment would be to bring peace through force of arms, but without the ability to shoot back unless absolutely necessary, and without all the necessary equipment. The enemy would be anybody who attacks. A risky assignment, and one that is unlikely to be acceptable politically.

There have been instances where officially sanctioned military operations have been undertaken to "make" peace, but on closer examination it is obvious these were mostly U.S. efforts with a cloak of approval from the United Nations, when they could possibly get it. This is not a hopeless situation—in fact quite the opposite. It is fairly clear that there is a role for outside interventions to help stop civil wars, and that the right strategy will go a long way to providing a way out for those locked in battle. But the delicate task, once there is an agreement, is to maneuver the two sides away from the short route back to war, an option as close, and within reach, as a gun at the hip.

Somalia in 1991 is an example of the problem with using UN forces to get two sides to stop fighting. Looking at what did not work well will not always point toward what does, but in this instance it will highlight the frightening ease with which trying to force peace can lead to disaster. The world community responded to a famine in Somalia, but eventually the clans began to interrupt international relief efforts. The warlords demanded payment in return for safe passage; at one point it appeared that relief agencies were feeding rival soldiers through a form of forced taxation. Eventually militias began to loot warehouses where food aid was stored. The process of trying to establish control caused a bloody mess as rival groups competed at the margins of their home turf. It was a situation that either someone needed to step into or relief agencies had to pull out of. It was into this chaos that the United States—at the request of the UN—attempted to inject peace. The book and movie *Black Hawk Down* have now etched the outcome in our memories. On that harrowing day in Mogadishu, American soldiers were caught in their own worst nightmare—downed, surrounded, and outnumbered by hostile locals.

It is an example of what could happen, and did happen, if we go too far to restore stability. In an attempt to impose order on a fractured country the United States found itself embroiled in the conflict we now know as "Somalia." The United States gave up and pulled its troops out, leaving the rubble to the UN to clean up. The role played by the United States came close to what the former under-secretary general of the United Nations advocated. More than a decade later Somalia remains caught up in instability, and all those difficult questions are still unanswered.

In April 1994 the genocide in Rwanda began to unfold. The UN had a contingent of peacekeepers on the ground. The commander, a Canadian, implored, pleaded, nearly begged the UN for help to cut short the efforts to organize the genocide. But nobody really listened. The UN knew something of very great magnitude was in the works. Although it had the time to get involved, the best attempt to prevent the genocide through negotiations and resolute action never got a hearing. As the killing started, ten Belgian peacekeepers became part of the casualty list, and there was no mistaking at this point just what was going on. You might think that when its own soldiers were killed the UN would rush in reinforcements to back up their troops on the ground and put down the unfolding carnage. Instead the only thing the UN could manage to do was to pull out all remaining peacekeepers, leaving the Tutsi at the mercy of the Hutus, who were bent on butchery. So close on the heels of Somalia, few political leaders were willing to incur the risk of another failure.

Somalia had demonstrated that order cannot be imposed in the midst of a civil war without a willingness to pay high costs in terms of treasure, blood, and prestige. The wrong lesson was learned from that debacle, contributing to the inaction over Rwanda three years after. It would be wrong, too, to walk away with the lesson that there is not a constructive role for the UN in the management of civil wars. Sir Brian Urquhart focused on the wrong set of policies, the wrong policy makers, and the wrong political institutions. The answer to the under-secretary general's question is an unequivocal yes: multilateral forces under the command of the United Nations do have a vital place in the management of civil wars. But not in the role of enforcer. The UN must play a role in keeping the peace once peace has been restored. But we cannot expect the UN to be the restorer of it in the first place.

B ecause of the frequency with which civil wars occur, it would be prudent to use the UN and other such institutions more effectively. There is an important role for peacekeepers at that point when, whether because of exhaustion or outside intervention, resolution to a war becomes a possibility. Peacekeepers can help organize and guarantee an acceptable outcome in civil wars that are on the verge of political settlements.

At the point where the rebel leadership is narrowing in on a peace agreement they can live with, they would have gained some concessions from the government. They would also have traded all the economic and political capital they could afford to. The agreement must undoubtedly have included provisions for the future of the rebel military force. The government will face the same issues with its own military. Without stipulations for a tangible outcome in this regard neither the government nor the rebel soldiers would be onboard with the agreement. Without disbanding and disarming the forces, without demobilization and the eventual integration of soldiers into civilian life, the country will still be left with two centers of authority, and at very best any agreement will then provide nothing more than an interlude between two periods of war.

If either side could have defeated the other, they would have. Make no mistake about that. If two sides are in negotiations—and in particular if they are nearly at the point of a signed agreement—it means that along with their fortunes on the battlefields, there exists a mutual understanding of the relative balance of each other's military capabilities. Outsiders can contribute to this balance, but in the end willingness to negotiate, make concessions, and sign an agreement reflects recognition that continued fighting was not going to achieve anything more than they could get at the negotiating table.

If these are the conditions under which two sides reach an agreement, why would a deal break down? Neither side, after all, won the war. Neither got everything they wanted. But in the end what they did get at the bargaining table must have been worth giving up fighting for. Enough people killed perhaps, enough villages tormented, and enough trauma visited upon the country brought both sides to the point of negotiations and agreement. However, too often agreements stop civil wars only for a brief time. A considerable number of all civil wars start up again after an agreement or a respite from the fighting.

The problems come from implementing certain aspects of an agreement. Transferring wealth or jobs might be easy when compared with demobilizing a rebel army and turning in weapons to the government. The weapons have to be collected, and caches destroyed. What might the government do then? The rebels have to hope that the government leadership is in the mood to be accommodating, because if not, it is likely to make sure the rebels are incapable of rising up again. Demobilization is critical to peace. But conditions have to be negotiated for rebels to be comfortable and secure demobilizing their forces. This has been a recurring problem with the IRA in Northern Ireland. They recognized the need to demobilize, but did not want to give up their secret arms caches without guarantees that ensure compliance by British and Loyalist forces. Once rebels give up their guns there is no turning back and no way to enforce violations that go against them. Without weapons not much stands between them and the gallows.

From the government's perspective the rebels waged war illegally, and are responsible for destroying the economy, driving investment capital out of the country, assassinating politicians, and destroying infrastructure. It would have considered the demands of the rebels too extreme, or would have granted them without a war, and anyone who challenged it before would remain a threat for the foreseeable future. With the rebels disarmed, there is nothing to stop government forces from arresting and killing all those who pose a continued threat. The government would finish what it couldn't during the war, ensuring that it would take some time before the opposition could raise an army again. At least this would be the fear of the rebels who fought against the government.

If the threat of force gives the government the incentive to follow through with terms of an agreement, the same is true in reverse.

If the government demobilized the army and police forces, rebels would be in a good position to take what they could not win at the bargaining table. Demobilization is particularly tricky because two sides that have been fighting a war obviously do not harbor a lot of trust for each other. And unlike in wars between two countries, in a civil war the two sides do not have separate countries to retreat to. They have to share the same piece of territory. Trust is important, disarmament is critical, and there is no unilateral incentive to spend too much energy on either.

There is a reason why this is a sticking point. Consider for a moment whether you would trust the government under these conditions by putting yourself in place of a soldier, villager, or parent who was caught up in the war. If your daughter, mother, wife, or sister was brutally raped by a group of government soldiers, how willing would you be to let it go? What if the rape was committed in front of you to make you betray your comrades? The same is true for the other side. A suicide bomber sidles up to a politician and blows everyone to bits, or gets on a bus full of children and turns it into an inferno. These memories and the hatred that accompanies them must be left behind before a new union and a new country can be built from the ashes of war. It is not easy. You need to overcome this to have the confidence to make peace.

To put this into perspective, many people see the death penalty as retribution for the heinous crimes of rape and murder. Not as a deterrent, but a way to "get back at the bastard" who did the horrible deed to someone they love. Multiply that grief, anger, and desire for revenge by your whole family or most of your village. This analogy illustrates in a personal way why it is so difficult to achieve a normal society after the trauma of a civil war. A peace agreement is a good first step, but an agreement is not peace, and any lull in the fighting it brings can be but temporary unless some important steps are taken that build confidence among communities. It is into such volatile and emotion-charged spaces that peacekeepers are called. Blue helmets, blue armbands, and a lot of distrusting, anger-filled people, many of whom want retribution. Not all of them do, but enough that it makes the transition very hard, and the peace rather fragile.

The focus must be on just what peacekeepers can do to overcome all of the limitations and liabilities that make their task perilous. Most peacekeeping forces, whether from the UN or from some other international organization, are made up of soldiers from many different countries that operate under a unified command structure. They are directed from an international or regional organization, and their assignments are of limited scope and duration. In short, they won't do too much, most of the time they won't stay too long, and their role will not be hijacked by any one country with a vested interest in the outcome. To agree to let them in, both sides would have to accept that they are there for the benefit of both, not to support one side over the other. And importantly, the peacekeepers are not all soldiers in the traditional sense. Some are law enforcement officials, some are bureaucrats, and some help train local people to demine fields and roads so that farming and transportation can resume.

Several books describe the activities of peacekeepers. Some are written from the perspective of an individual peacekeeper, some from that of a particular peacekeeping mission, and some from the vantage point of the entire UN peacekeeping program. My task is much more modest and yet more sweeping. I do not see using UN forces as the bulwark against insurgencies the world over. This would put the UN in the position of effectively taking on the role of the host government. Neither can I envision UN forces siding with rebels to overthrow a sitting government. This would make the UN too much of a threat to all governments. UN peacekeeping forces must engage in the vital task of keeping peace once it has been restored. This involves doing whatever is necessary to help make the transition from war to peace.

I have never been a peacekeeper, observed a peacekeeping operation firsthand, or even interviewed commanders of peacekeeping units. My understanding of peacekeepers in the role of marshalling peace agreements toward peace and stability comes from academic studies. My friend's father was a lieutenant colonel in the Norwegian army and served as a peacekeeper in Gaza and in Lebanon. He was in Lebanon during 1985 and 1986, a period that I know was rough: Israelis had invaded from the south, and there was a civil war in the north. This period also followed shortly on the heels of the massacre of Palestinians at the Shatila and Sabra refugee camps, and the bombing of the U.S. marine barracks in Beirut in which 183 marines were killed. It could not have been an easy task to keep peace in this environment.

In order to get a sense from someone who has been there, I asked him if he would sit down with me to recount some of his experiences as a peacekeeper. I wanted to ask him what worked to defuse tension and how the peacekeepers responded under fire. I was looking for any incidents and insights that would help illuminate, at a more personal level, the task of peacekeepers. I was looking for excitement, thrills, and tales of daring and danger. Lieutenant Colonel Karlson, though, never saw a hostile moment during his tour of duty in Lebanon. He thought that that was as it should be. I was looking for drama, he talked about the mundane. Tea and biscuits with local people was among the more memorable parts of his job. There were times when he talked people out of harsh acts, but mostly his role was just to be there. I was puzzled at first, but then came to realize that he is right. He kept the peace by being peaceful, by being visible, and by communicating with members of the community.

Of course, not all peacekeeping missions were tea and biscuits in Lebanon. In fact over the twenty-year operation in Lebanon, two hundred and fifty peacekeepers were killed. Sometimes they were direct targets, sometimes unintended ones. But to Lieutenant Colonel Karlson his job revolved around instilling confidence—confidence that agreements would be implemented, confidence that one side could withdraw without the opponent taking advantage. This is the core of the problem faced by the rebel and government leaders at the point of an agreement. Both sides are wound into a vicious cycle of mutual distrust, mutual antagonisms, and mutual recriminations. Even if they prefer an end to the hostilities they have a difficult time taking the steps necessary to get there. They cannot commit to do that which they prefer to do.

To make peace and rebuild the country the war must stop, and the major players cannot be left in a position where restarting it is the best option. The mechanisms that make war possible must be removed at the same time that the social infrastructure is rebuilt. Both sides must have the incentives and the resources to remake relationships that led to war in the first place. The government confronts an enormous task and it needs the support of the opposition to rebuild the country, the economy, the social infrastructure, and the political mechanisms. Each has been torn asunder by the war, and each is critical to sustaining peace. To rebuild the economy the government has to have access to money. Aid would be welcome, but ultimately there has to be money to invest in economic development. To rebuild the social infrastructure requires money, popular support, and technical help. The same is true of the political machinery and the economic foundation of the country.

Somebody has to guarantee that the process unfolds as it was laid out in the peace treaty. Although both sides are disarming they have to be confident that someone will occupy the void that results. The most obvious void is military security, but domestic instability, the lack of institutions to distribute resources, and a pervasive sense of distrust also pose serious problems for implementation.

People are hurting at the end of a war. They are broke, some seek revenge, many are scared. What the people of Iraq feared most after the U.S. invasion was criminal activity. They were fearful in spite of the fact that there were one hundred and fifty thousand U.S. troops on the ground! Political leaders often have various police forces that operate at their command—treasury police, palace police, and military police. In the U.S. there are local and state police; Alcohol, Tobacco, and Firearms police (ATF); FBI; and the U.S. Citizenship and Immigration Service (USCIS); all of which have a role in enforcing U.S. laws. Soldiers and the police force play different roles in society, but sometimes in the midst of a civil war the police end up doing the work of the military. They are the ones carrying out arrests, torture, and disappearances throughout the countryside. When the average person cannot trust the police, the police lose authority. The forces have to be purged and new officers trained. This is one of the major tasks of the United States in the rebuilding of Iraq. Only an outside group can train a new police force.

If you start taking apart the police force, criminals can too easily wreak havoc on society, and at a time when law and order is more important than ever. The rebels cannot accept the police force as it stands, but neither can society accept the void created by dissolution of the force. Peacekeepers fulfill this role quite effectively. When the UN sent a peacekeeping force into Cambodia at the end of that conflict, about a quarter of it was assigned to supervise Cambodia's 50,000 civilian police officers. The force was composed of 3,600 monitors, about one international police officer overseeing fifteen Cambodian ones. Without this UN oversight it is unlikely that different factions within the country would have had confidence in the national civilian police. And if the streets are not safe, there cannot be progress on economic reconstruction or political changes that are required for full participation. Just contributing to the policing capabilities does not resolve problems of demobilization or attitudes and perceptions of distrust, but it helps in many ways.

If implementation of a peace agreement hinges on the reorganization of the police force, then the UN stepping into that breach can be crucial. This does not mean that the UN has to occupy every police position. Ideas about attitudes and acceptable practices are handed down from above. The police on the street get their cues from the commander in the station, or from the political leadership. U.S. soldiers' treatment of the prisoners at the Abu Ghraib prison in Iraq and the Guantánamo Bay prison in Cuba is a recent example. It is the soldier who is being prosecuted for those actions, but there is clearly enough evidence to show that those at the top—the very top—considered a little torture acceptable. The peacekeepers' job is to change the attitudes of those on the lower end of the law enforcement hierarchy by removing, replacing, and retraining those at the top.

Even with good supervision of the local police, demobilization will remain a critical step in the implementation of a peace agreement. The rebels are still not going to give up their weapons very easily. The police are underarmed relative to the military, so if the rebels give up their guns before the government's army does, they are putting themselves in a tight spot because the police are in no position to ensure their safety. Demobilization has to occur simultaneously, or at least under the protection and supervision of a neutral force. Confidence in compliance is a must, as is the guarantee that there will be no exploitation. In effect, there has to be a guarantee of security before disarmament can take place. The 2005 agreement to end the civil war in southern Sudan is a prime example. The agreement that has ended over twenty years of civil war does not require the disarmament of the rebel militia for six years! Obviously the rebels lack any confidence that the government will follow through with its obligations, and they have good reason. The government reneged on the previous agreement that almost ended the war, right after the rebels disarmed. The rebels won't be fooled again. In most cases a six-year disarmament period just doesn't happen, because any one country cannot for long sustain two competing armies vying for allegiance and control. In Sudan the government was willing to agree because it so desperately needed to stop the war.

Demobilizing an army is not straightforward. The logistical issues multiply as you begin to think about the entire process of demobilization. For instance, to whom do you give your weapons? The government is the recognized center of authority in the country and the rebels have signed a deal that codifies this relationship. But do you think for a moment that the rebel leaders are going to march their troops down to the local army barracks and hand over their weapons? After fighting a war in which they were not defeated it would be very unlikely that they would take such a step. One way to think of this is as voluntary demobilization, a part of the peace process. Another, however, is as a way of arming your enemy. That isn't going to happen at this point in the tense relationship between the rebels and the government.

Questions of demobilization can be framed in terms of a fundamental security problem, one in which neither side has a way to guarantee the security of the other. It is partially those entrenched animosities that linger after the destruction, abuse, and death that come with civil war that make this implementation stage so difficult. To get out of this conundrum requires guarantees, security, and compliance. Someone from the outside must provide these necessary conditions.

Even though these conditions are necessary for securing the peace, it is not necessary that the United Nations be responsible.

Whatever organization does provide the guarantees has to be seen as impartial, but it could be any of a number of others that could ensure compliance: the African Union, NATO, the Organization of American States, or the European Union. The UN happens to be a good role model for this task, and one that draws its forces from several different countries. It has not only developed a workable strategy, but can pass the impartiality test.

When we hear of *peacekeepers, UN observers,* and the like, they are really catchall terms used to describe the many roles performed by the Blue Helmeted forces. Getting weapons out of the hands of suspicious soldiers is a logistically and psychologically delicate operation. At a minimum they need a central place where the weapons can be brought for "decommissioning." This allows peacekeepers to provide security while arms are being turned in. They find a location that can represent a safe haven, a staging area where troops can congregate and feel comfortable giving up their guns. The peace agreement might stipulate that forces are to congregate at one of these areas to turn in weapons, a security zone where the UN is the dominant force. The UN is there to accept, catalog, and cart away the vast array of guns, ammo, and heavy equipment that are turned over. But most importantly they are there to provide security while the process is going on. Because of the lack of trust, small violations in a cease-fire can result in the near-total breakdown of the demobilization process. Security is important.

To give an idea of the size of the demobilization process, at the end of the Nicaraguan civil war the UN set up a number of security zones to collect the weapons of the rebels. A total of 19,614 rebels showed up at the zones in Nicaragua over the course of two months. They turned in over 15,000 small arms, including AK-47s and other automatic weapons, missiles, heavy machine guns, and mortars. Importantly, the soldiers who turned in their guns were helped to resettle in development zones where they could be put to work in more constructive pursuits. At the end of the Cambodian civil war the UN moved over 50,000 of the opposing forces into security zones as part of the demobilization process. This task is not easy, but it is critically important to making the peace last.

The rebel leadership also has to have the confidence that the conditions that led them to take up arms in the first place will not continue to be part of the political and economic landscape of the country. From a military vantage point they have waged war and were not defeated, and this almost entitles them to some concessions from the government. Without any concessions they might as well have continued fighting. In order to ensure some form of structural change the rebels will undoubtedly have demanded political reforms that provide them with access to the political system. This will entail a more inclusive legislative body, and potentially equal access to the prospects for political leadership. This might mean turning the rebel movement into a political party, but in return there is some chance that this party will generate political representation. In effect the reforms will reflect changes toward a more open political system, one that includes representatives from the rebel organization. There are numerous other conditions that form the backbone of any peace agreement: the distribution of resources, the size of the government's military, the role of domestic police, and so on. The devil, here, is not in the details but in the implementation of the details in the peace agreement.

An open and inclusive political process might be the salvation for countries negotiating an end to a civil war, even though at the time there would appear to be more pressing concerns. Both the government and the rebels will have learned something about the role of power in getting political and economic access. The rebels have recognized that a large part of the problem that led to the war in the first place is that they were cut out of the political process. The neglect and abuse that caused the war were partially a result of people not being politically powerful enough to get a fair deal within the political system. If the war ended in a negotiated settlement it would have taught them that military power can be turned into political power, and then into economic access. Those who challenged the government are stronger because they took up arms and could not be defeated. The last thing they would want to do is give up that power and access by giving up their weapons and getting nothing in return. We already know that.

How, then, do the rebels ensure that what they won by war will remain through times of peace? The answer is political access. If the rebels were strong enough militarily to fight the government to a draw, they must have enough supporters to become a real political force. They have a claim to access to the political system.

The best way to get into the system is through democratic reforms. This is not the only way, but certainly one that will help ensure that future political arrangements will not lead to the types of oppression that convinced farmers and laborers to take up arms. Getting into the political process means political parties, registered voters, publicity, making sure those who fought feel secure about registering and participating. If those who ran the country before the war are responsible for the mechanics of political inclusion, rebels and their supporters will be suspicious and may stay away. If they do, the old government will win any political contest and have the right to claim political legitimacy. This could translate into a mandate to rule, and by extension a mandate to go back to the old ways. The war would have been for naught and the new arrangements will remain tenuous. A new war might always loom over the horizon.

I think back to the leaders of the support group for the Mothers of the Disappeared in Guatemala. Just being in the same room with them, in all honesty, scared the hell out of me. I was constantly afraid that the security forces would consider me a collaborator. Being in this situation is akin to being with someone buying drugs, knowing someone who committed a crime, attending a meeting that is bordering on illegal. It can be nerve-wracking to be in constant fear that the door will be kicked in. My friends in Guatemala had organized *because* the door had already been kicked in, and one of their relatives disappeared with the soldiers who left! My feeling is that they became inured to the fear. But they never lost sight of why they were putting themselves at such risk, and they did not lose sight of it at the end of the war either. They knew they needed to be part of the political process, and to do that they needed guarantees that they would be included. It is all tied up with surrendering weapons, but it is more than that. A political process must be put in place. The opposition at this point is not in the position to leave it to the goodwill of the government to put in place the mechanisms that open up the political process. The UN or other outside organizations can help. With somebody watching over the transition from war to peace it is much more difficult for people to renege on an agreement.

At this point, when the economy is probably in trouble and the government needs an infusion of cash to help turn things around, reneging can be very costly. The last thing either the government or the rebels want is aid, trade, and investment walking away. This gives a point of leverage that the UN and others can exploit. The UN has vast technical capabilities to help build a political process, and building a legitimate political system requires such technical help. Starting a political party or running an effective campaign or a voter registration drive are all more easily done by having someone onboard who knows the ropes. The leader of the rebellion may have been a good commander but may not be a good politician or political strategist. Right at the start the former rebels are at a great disadvantage relative to those who supported the government. The UN can provide this technical expertise and has demonstrated it in such situations around the world.

If the rebel leadership senses that they have at least a chance in the political process they will be much more comfortable putting down the only security they have—the gun. At a very simple level the world community can send in people to observe the fairness of the political process that determines who rules after the war. Election observers come from everywhere, every walk of life, and every political stripe. The impact of election observers is by no means minimal. Take Victor Yushchenko, the man who was elected prime minister of Ukraine in 2004. The political machinery of the government apparently stole the election from the opposition. International election observers cried foul, and this gave moral authority to the opposition candidate to call his supporters out into the streets. The results of the fraudulent election were overturned. If you are the opposition, someone looking over the shoulder of those who have most of the control over the election process may be your most important asset at the time.

Reliable police, demobilization, and a more transparent political process are all vital to maintain the peace. Each addresses one element of the power relationship between government and rebels, and taken together they can be enough to convince each side that the civil war is over. None of them, however, deals with the individual or national pain of war. To many who deal with questions of reconciliation, before there can be peace there must be tears, tears of healing and tears of forgiving.

If the story of civil wars is about poverty, discrimination, and brutality, then ending the motivation for them must also be about those things. But my mind always returns to the forty thousand women and girls raped in the Congolese civil war, to the use of rape in the Bosnian and Kosovo civil wars of the 1990s, and to the utter brutality of the governments of El Salvador, Guatemala, Chile, and Argentina. It is one thing to fight a war to change the way resources are distributed; it is yet another to experience the total disregard for humanity from your opponent. Getting over a civil war can require putting humanity back into the relationship between the power brokers and those who fought them. Without it animosities will linger, peace will be fragile, and any violation of a peace agreement will seem like a frontal assault.

The American Civil War seems like a long way off to most of us. If you are from the North you probably know the story of Sherman's march to the sea as a great military victory where the Union army defeated the Confederates once and for all. The victory ensured the unity of the Union. If you are from the South you've probably heard the stories quite differently. The Union soldiers under the command of Sherman plundered and pillaged the countryside. They left nothing standing. To some from the South it was a brutal and unnecessary abuse of power. One hundred fifty years later you can still feel traces of that Civil War lingering in the attitudes and impressions of people in both the North and the South. In country after country the abuses that take place during civil wars leave little to the imagination. To get past this terrible legacy of the country's history it sometimes requires confronting openly the abuses that are part of that history.

One tool for the cleansing that is often required to make the country whole again is a "truth commission." Not everybody likes a truth commission, because it tends to let the guilty go free. But the evidence might convince you that letting the guilty and the plundered tell their story can help bring fractured communities back together. A truth commission is very different from an amnesty given out by the government to military and political leaders who are undoubtedly guilty of crimes. In the former it is the community that accepts and tries to forgive. In the latter it is the ruling group that hides behind its own power. One helps cleanse, the other allows wounds to fester. Nelson Mandela realized that for South Africa to heal, the oppressed would have to work to free the oppressors, that those who imprisoned him were also, in a sense, imprisoned in their history of abuse, perpetrated in the name of maintaining privilege.

A truth commission is a mechanism allowing for a common view of the history of the war. At the end of a war the two sides still have to live in the same country with the same government. There is no avoiding this commingling of former enemies. A truth commission allows all people to hear the story of the war from the perspective of those who suffered as well as from those who were the instruments of the suffering. By telling the story, describing the abuse, recalling and recounting the activities, identifying the torturers, and in effect asking your compatriots for forgiveness, attitudes about what happened and why can be changed. This is what truth commissions can facilitate. They can't undo the damage, they can't give back a life, and they can't rebuild the economy. But they can help rebuild the nation, help mend the fractures along lines of religion, ethnicity, language, or class. Truth commissions can make it more difficult to go back to war by replacing private accountability with a collective sense of the wrongs done in the name of war. Private accountability is vengeance. Collective accountability can facilitate healing.

There are many different ways to lay bare the record of a country's abuse in war. If it is at the end of a victorious war, this process is often organized as war crimes tribunals. Not quite the same as a truth commission, but a way of getting out as much information as possible about abuses, and ultimately punishing those responsible. Tribunals are tools of the victors over the vanquished. Rwanda has held trials for the perpetrators of the genocide. At the World Court in The Hague, former leaders of the Yugoslav regime are on trial for crimes in Bosnia and Kosovo. There is always a victor-vanquished relationship to these trials. In the end, punishment will be meted out to the guilty, who at times are guilty by definition because they lost the war.

When a peace agreement is what stops a civil war, tribunals may be less relevant than truth commissions. These can be set up as part of the peace accord itself, may be organized by internal political processes, or may be unofficial bodies to explore past abuses. El Salvador had a truth commission mandated as part of the peace accord that brought an end to the war. South Africa established its own Truth and Reconciliation Commission. In Guatemala a truth commission was established by the Catholic Church. In each case the task of the commission was to investigate human rights abuses that took place during the war. There is always a risk to the abusers from admitting their atrocities publicly, but the idea behind the commissions is predicated on the notion of collective absolution. But just as there is a risk to the guilty, many of the victims see truth commissions as a way to let the guilty off without punishment. In South Africa many of the organizers of the abuse of blacks confessed their guilt in front of the commission and were officially forgiven for their crimes. To those who suffered it does not always seem fair. The key is to get past the individual vengeance and accept collective responsibility.

When I think of reconciliation I try to imagine watching my mother or sister raped, a friend bound and mutilated, a brother disappearing one night. Could I get past that just because the guilty admitted guilt? I am against the death penalty, and always have been. I once volunteered to be the coordinator for an anti–death penalty campaign in Detroit. Part of that task involved a public debate with a proponent of the death penalty. I had heard his case many times— mostly I thought it was about retribution. During a question-and-answer period someone described to me a horrific hypothetical rape and murder of my spouse and the kidnapping of my children. Then he asked me if I would support the death penalty under such conditions. I said no because I honestly didn't think that taking yet another life would make anything better. I was booed and hissed at by the crowd, called uncaring, unhuman, and unbelievable. I was perplexed, but I thought about the hypothetical event on my drive home. Would I really want to see the person who did that to my family executed? I started to think that maybe I would.

I learned something about retribution from a friend. Marietta, then a young parent, was camping with her family, the kids in one tent and the parents in another. In the middle of the night someone sliced through the side of the kids' tent and took her five-year-old daughter. It took a year, but they eventually found the man who kidnapped and murdered Susie. Marietta met with the man and reconciled with him the mutual tragedies they faced. Susie's murderer killed himself in jail but Marietta keeps in touch with his parents. Both families have suffered tragic losses, and harboring a desire for retribution was not going to help Marietta get on with life. I don't know that I would be as strong as Marietta, but I am convinced that she is healthier and more secure in life because of her approach to her daughter's tormentor. That image has stuck with me, and I can only imagine the horrors that are suffered by those in the midst of a civil war. There are a number of studies that demonstrate that the recovery process is hastened if the victims begin to care more about reconciliation than retribution, and truth commissions provide one of the best ways to do so.

Fighting a war is traumatic; finding an acceptable peace agreement to end the war is difficult. But making the peace stick might be the hardest part of all. If the participants have worked hard to get the peace agreement, they owe it to themselves to turn that agreement into an agenda that can work. According to research by Barbara Walter, a professor of political science at UC San Diego, nearly 50 percent of all negotiated agreements are never implemented. The peace deals break down. The road to peace is littered with issues of getting both sides past the trauma, past the distrust, and past uncertainty for the future. Taking up this gauntlet is a vital task for the world community. The United Nations is the organization best suited to do so. Private voluntary organizations can help, as can individual governments. But at the core many of the roles necessary to maintain the peace require integrity, objectivity, and impartiality, which are all attributes of the UN.

We have learned a lot in the fifteen or so years since Under-Secretary General Urquhart asked the question "Isn't there something that we can do?" The answer I give is not the one he advocated, but it is an answer that suggests that we do not have to sit back and watch the carnage on television. First, there has to be the political will to act. Then, policies must be designed that stand a reasonable chance of success. If negotiations and incentives can get those fighting a civil war to seek a peace agreement, the adroit use of our global resources can help them secure the peace they seek. Disarmament, security, political access, and truth commissions will not reverse all the problems that led to armed rebellion in the first place, but they do give those who chose the path of rebellion the means to move beyond war.

14

◆ ◆ ◆

THE ROAD TO DAMASCUS

Thirty years ago Cambodia shocked me into realizing the brutality of civil wars and their aftermath. At the time, I could only think of going there to help alleviate the trauma of the famine that followed. I now hold an entirely different perspective, one born of scholarly inquiry and more mellowed reasoning. But I still can't shake the overarching conclusion that such levels of carnage are unwarranted and unnecessary, and that what we do matters. The images I saw then, of people fleeing from war into camps or the countryside only to find life precarious if not utterly bleak, I still see today in the Congo, Darfur, Sri Lanka, and the Philippines. And I need look no further than the carnage in Iraq to say that today's generation has its civil war. I started this book by asking what it would take to get you to take up arms against your government. I wanted you to think about how thin the line is that separates each of us from those people in the Congo or Sudan. On most dimensions, the Blacks of Darfur were just like you and me until resources started getting scarce, and until the competition for those resources began to get violent. We all strive to live life just as long and as fruitfully as we can, and this makes the person in Sudan not so very different from the person in New York. We learned long ago that the blood of a black man flows effortlessly through the veins of a white one, and the heart of one works just as well in the other. None of us anywhere in the world is completely immune from the trauma of civil war.

As individuals we can and most often do sit by and live our lives oblivious to the daily horrors faced by some, but as a community of people we are uneasy about this response. National leaders squirm at the thought of doing nothing, even though trying to figure out the "right" response makes them squirm even more. Rwanda taught us that lesson.

We confront at this point one of those moral dilemmas that give academics pause, spiritual leaders fodder for the pulpit, and the political and economic elite a moment to reflect. As a scholar I am not very taken by moral imperatives; politics happens for political reasons, often driven by self-interest. But as a member of our global village I do confront the question of what the "right" thing to do is. In our increasingly interconnected world there must be a way for political and economic leaders to be political, for spiritual leaders to be moral, for academics to square evidence with argument, and still do the right thing for the well-being and security of our fellow citizens of the world. When I first learned about the Cambodian famine and civil war, I wanted to drop everything and go there to help. What seemed right to me was driven by an altruistic impulse and intuition. Years of studying civil wars did not fundamentally change what I see as the right thing to do, that niggling moral imperative, but only how to do it. My running off to Cambodia wasn't going to change things very much, and I think evidence would support that conclusion. But there are things that we as a community can do to change the course of events that compel people to force change through violence. I'm not suggesting silver bullets or quixotic campaigns, but rather a reorientation of how we square political and economic distributions with our willingness to tolerate political violence.

There is a model in vogue of a globalized world, an interconnected economic structure that advances the fortunes of all. But this model must confront its detractors, who point to the unrestricted market as the cause of political turmoil, not the solution. The disparity in wealth between rich and poor countries is partially a result of colonialism, during which exploitation was the norm. Some see globalization as the modern version of colonial exploitation, in which unfettered markets take what is no longer acceptable to take through military conquest. The rich—and the advocates of an open economy—get richer while many of the rest slip closer to, or further into, poverty.

The mortgage crisis of 2008 is the middle-class American version of this nightmare playing out while the rapes and murders in Darfur, the Congo, and Iraq mount. The managers of the U.S. economic system are trying desperately to infuse money into the Western banking system in order to stave off financial instability. You could draw parallels to the Argentinean crisis of 2001, though the consequences would be much more dire. I think I have made the case that it is partially a fault in the system that pushes people like you and me to consider taking up a gun.

A friend of mine, a Catholic bishop, is wont to say that God did not create this world for the few to have far too much while the many have far too little. From a spiritual perspective this poses the moral dilemma of poverty in a world of plenty. From a political perspective this lays the foundation for instability and civil war. By my reading of political and historical events the economic elite understand this.

The elite of the political and business world gather each year at an economic summit in Davos, Switzerland. The purpose of this meeting is to examine ways to improve the state of the world, at least in terms of how its stability affects the business climate. The agenda at the 2005 meeting focused on tackling "the tough issues of poverty, climate change, education, equitable globalization and good global governance." Public figures, from diplomats to rock stars, took up that call for the elimination of global poverty. Nelson Mandela called for wealthy countries to write off the debt of poor ones. Bono appeals to our conscience to be the generation that makes poverty history, using words like "scandal" to describe the lack of action on the part of the policy community and the public in the Western industrialized countries—us. I point this out to suggest that elimination of poverty has been raised to the level of the moral responsibility of the wealthy. However you choose to take these ideas, it is clear that poverty in poor countries is not going away unless those in wealthy countries help make it happen. Since poverty is at the foundation of many of the civil wars in the world, reducing poverty will reduce the number of civil wars. If the people at the World Economic Forum could achieve their goals, we might actually have found the way to dramatically reduce them.

Reducing poverty to a level that reduces the motivation to rebel against a government will take an effort by wealthy and poor countries alike. This does not mean that the wealthy must become poor so that the poor are poor no more, but there is certainly a necessity for an economic system that is not stacked against those living in the poor countries of the world. At least some of the people attending the Forum in Davos recognized this. But in response to Nelson Mandela's call for debt relief the United States implicated the governments in the poor countries. It is not the debt per se, said the Bush administration, but corruption and poor government in the poorest countries that keep them where they are. There is no doubt that corruption is rampant in the poorer countries—as well as in some of the wealthier ones. But dismissing the need for action and responsibility by pointing the finger at those countries that need the most help is not productive. Nor does it do much for the image of the strong in the eyes of the weak.

It is naive, however, to think that poverty and hunger can be ended, or that the problem is just one of knowledge and information. I once worked with an antihunger organization in New York City, educating high school students about issues of global hunger. These jobs are intense, energy-consuming positions for which maintaining morale is a critical aspect of managerial strategies. One of our meetings started with a morale-boosting exercise. Around the table were some twenty-five people who came from distinguished walks of life. There were professors, CEOs, managers, leaders of nonprofit organizations, and then me, the T-shirt and sandals among suits. The leader of the meeting asked us to describe what we thought it would be like when poverty and hunger had ended. I listened to some very smart people saying some pretty outlandish things that day—there would be flowers blooming everywhere, the sun would shine for weeks, homeless shelters would disappear. It went on. I was the last to speak, and I was uneasy. I felt out of my league, and, in truth, I couldn't see the end of poverty. I expressed my opinion that hunger will persist, that there was not enough political will to end it, and that even if flowers bloomed in New York City, Lagos and Calcutta would still have street people. Poverty would not be eliminated in the idealist sense, I said, but chronic structural poverty could be reduced substantially. The group continued to invite me to future meetings, though I never really understood why.

I set out with the objective of linking arguments, intuition, and evidence about civil wars to make clear why they start and how they stop. I developed my explanation for civil wars by asking you to think about conditions under which you, you personally, would leave your job, family, and home to take up the life of a rebel soldier fighting to change your government. I realize that this is a difficult question to contemplate, let alone answer definitively. If we assume that you *could* join an armed insurrection, at least in principle, the important question is *when* you would. I suspect that in the face of some strong motivations you would tell yourself to give the system one more chance, just one more. What would finally push you to join the rebellion?

Most countries were founded on some sort of revolutionary behavior, and many of our forebears did join rebellions. In the United States, according to some, it is the obligation to overthrow a tyrannical government that enshrines your right to own guns in the Constitution. So not only is it thinkable; the Constitution actually provides the access to weapons and the obligation. Would being poor be enough to push you over that edge? I doubt it. Most wealthy countries rarely let the poor be poor enough, and when they do, their numbers are too small and their capabilities too limited to become a serious threat. In poorer countries there are more poor people and their governments are more likely to abuse them. This volatile mix, as we know, can breed disaster. Poverty is not a necessary condition for civil war, but it is a frequent one in countries that are at war. And, are there conditions under which you would choose to shoot at the soldiers of your own country rather than side with them? There are. You just have to look deeply to find them. But having identified those conditions, it is still a long road to civil war.

Different scholars come up with different explanations for why poverty might lead to civil war, but the causal mechanisms are somewhat less important than the fact that poverty *is* at the core of most civil wars. Poverty is not an absolute concept. There is not some standard below which you are impoverished. If you have ever experienced poverty you know what I am talking about. Real poverty is something that you can feel, smell, sense. It is not just being broke, or having a hard time making both the car payment and the house payment this month. Poverty grinds. Widespread poverty is a result of a whole country being poor, as in countries that are not able to generate enough resources for all to share. Poverty can be the result of corruption—sometimes poor countries generate resources but a few squander the resources of the many. You can be poor in a rich country, or you can be poor in a poor country. Whether the link between poverty and civil war is found in the inability of governments to respond to challenges, or provides the motivation for people to rise up, doesn't really matter that much either. Even if a government has the capability to confront a rebel army, poverty will always give the opposition motivation to rebel. Structural poverty—poverty born of discrimination—is that grinding poverty that can motivate individuals to take risks they might otherwise avoid. If you've seen it, experienced it, breathed it, you understand how it strips away dignity. People might not always choose the armed route, but the incentives will be there. To eliminate civil war you have to address issues of structural poverty. Global, national, and local poverty.

I have studied civil wars for over a decade and the evidence as I read it points to that one overarching problem: structural poverty. It may be that structural poverty results from exploitation, greed, the market system, globalization, or some or all of these, and this remains an open and complicated question. There is some evidence that globalization—that freewheeling market system that opens everything to everybody—is related to more violence within countries. Globalization might lead to greater disparity between the well-off and the less well-off. Certainly if the advocates of globalization didn't think that the process would generate wealth for them, they would not be such strong advocates of it. Their common logic is that the rising tide will raise all ships. I don't know. What I do know is that there is an alternative way to see the world, particularly as it pertains to impoverishment. In Calcutta, the more I walked the streets, the more people I saw living and dying in the gutters; the more often I carried the dead out the back door of the Home for the Destitute, the more puzzled I became. I could not understand what had gripped this wonderful city in a way that has happened to no other city I had ever seen. Nowhere else that I had been could Mother Teresa have set up a home for the destitute and dying and have people banging on the doors to get in with such regularity.

I spent afternoons in Calcutta just walking the streets and talking to people. I eventually began to ask why this level of human misery happens in Calcutta, and almost only Calcutta. The answer that I always got, and I mean always, was that it was because West Bengal, of which Calcutta is the capital, is a communist state. Not the market, not globalization, but communism. To some it is the market, to others it is the lack of a market. I don't profess to know the answers to global poverty, nor is that the objective of this book. What is clear to me is that if we want to reduce the number of civil wars, we must address those factors that motivate normal people to adopt an abnormal and risky strategy for change. Structural poverty at the national and international levels is front and center.

The solutions to poverty are probably much more complex than the processes of civil wars. But if you can conclude that widespread poverty and desperation are at the core of tens of millions of people dying from hunger, and that poverty can be found at the root of most civil wars that kill and maim millions, then it behooves us to think about solutions defined in terms of poverty. We can't easily walk away from that unless we are willing to conclude that the problem of civil wars is not our problem. Few policy makers actually come to that conclusion, at least publicly.

It is hard for me as a social scientist to talk about moral imperatives. But we cannot consider the problem of civil wars without confronting the implications of what we know about them. And it seems to me that we do have a moral imperative to work toward eliminating poverty. Even if you reject the notion of moral imperatives, the wealthy, market-efficient countries have a strategic interest in reducing poverty because it will reduce the frequency of civil wars. Either way, if your focus is on the scourge of civil war, there is every reason to applaud the agenda of the 2005 World Economic Forum in Davos, Switzerland; to support the call of the rock star Bono; and to act on the pleas of many in the poorer parts of the world.

I am many things but naive is not one of them. I do not think there will be daisies blooming the day poverty ends. I do not believe that we really can formally end poverty. There is a need to be realistic about the range of possible outcomes. The world can take a lot of steps to reduce the number of people who live at the margins, but eliminating poverty like polio or smallpox would be a different task. The corrupt government and the corrupt individual, corporate greed, drug addiction and alcoholism, old age, poor health, odd inheritance policies, and the rules that determine how goods and services are exchanged all contribute to poverty. But so too does structural discrimination. The structural and distributional problems are the ones that can be addressed at the national and international levels. It is the way poverty plays out within a particular society that is most problematic. When the poverty is restricted primarily to one group, the motivations to rise up become more acute. It only takes someone who thinks changes must be made and who can organize an opposition movement and energize a group of people. But this great organizer cannot organize anybody unless he has a grievance against his government. Poverty, economic distress, and life at the margins are a very strong grievance.

Even if the world were to reject the call from the World Economic Forum leaders, pay no attention to an activist rock star, and ignore Nelson Mandela's urging of leaders to address poverty through debt relief, there is still another route out of the civil war dilemma. We don't have to eliminate poverty to reduce the frequency of civil war. We could just reduce the motivation to move beyond nonviolent protest into armed rebellion. I stressed early on that poverty is not a sufficient condition to create civil wars. A lot of other factors have to come into play. Bad government policy is one of them. Consider for a moment that you are impoverished in America. You would like the situation to change in your favor, and you might even join an opposition group that helps press your case. There are many poor folks in America and a number of groups working to better the conditions of the poor. The difference between these groups in America and those in Sudan, India, or Sri Lanka is found in how tolerant the government is to political demands. The evidence points to government response as the culprit in turning dissension into armed rebellion. Better politics would turn heads, and many will champion the cause of democracy in their answer.

Perhaps there is no moral imperative to reduce poverty, but rather one to promote democracy. Certainly there are some advocates of this position. To reduce the number of civil wars, those governments that face challenges from organized opposition groups must refrain from abusing their opponents. A little bit of repression appears to quell the ambitions of those who are less committed to a cause. Repressing the opposition also seems to act like an opiate on the repressors. Once you violate the norms of society it is hard to ease back on the impulses to do so. When something works you tend to want to go back to that strategy. But governments make choices over whether to accommodate groups or repress them. Far too often the easiest choice appears to be repression. This happens in democracies, but less frequently than under other forms of government. When faced with a challenge, democratic leaders will also resort to a repressive policy rather than an accommodative one. In early 2005, British prime minister Tony Blair publicly apologized for the wrongful imprisonment of the Guildford Four and the Maguire Seven. These men were convicted of IRA bombings in the struggle over Northern Ireland. The British got the wrong guys. In effect they were political prisoners. The British probably wanted them out of the way, and jailing them proved to be one method. The cases of these men helped solidify the opposition.

My reading of the evidence points to smart government policies as one of the keys to minimizing the pool of potential rebel soldiers. What is not clear is whether democracy provides enough of this enlightened leadership. Britain and Spain have each used political assassination as a tool in their wars against the IRA and the Basques, respectively. We now know that the Bush administration condoned the use of violent means of coercion—torture—as long as it did not approach the point where the subject felt death was imminent. Israel uses torture and political assassinations to counter the threat it faces from the Palestinians, and I doubt that you would want to be a political prisoner in India. Democratic government is not the only aspect of good government policy that is important.

To reduce the chances that any one individual will be pushed toward a rebel group, governments have to be tolerant. Tolerant of opposition demands, tolerant of their techniques, and tolerant of issues related to their group identity. It might be easy to suggest that opposition groups also have to be tolerant, and should temper the fervor with which they press their demands so as not to force the hand of the government. I would be more inclined to make restraint and toleration the responsibility of the government. The opposition early on generally has few weapons, they are not organized for violence, and they actually think they might get some concessions through protest. The initial protest is often legal. The government is much more secure and has numerous options to channel dissent into a constructive role. In fact, if the opposition reaches the point of public protest and demonstrations, the government probably has some serious room for reform.

Governments have to be tolerant, and at the beginning they have all the power and probably feel no need to make concessions. But by not compromising they place themselves into a vicious spiral. They use repressive violence that angers more of the people, which requires more repression, which leads the opposition to advocate armed struggle. The willingness to debate over disagreements about the way resources are distributed would forestall much of the incentive for the opposition to take up arms. Not giving an inch on the basis that demands will never stop is a silly way to run a government. The downside costs of a civil war, after all, are so much greater than the costs of making some of the easy concessions. Yes, there are political constituencies on both sides, but political leaders are supposed to lead, and not lead the country into a civil war.

What I find rather odd about government behavior is that the citizens' demands could come as a surprise to the leadership. The leaders of government seem to have little understanding about the grievances of their citizens and their willingness to endure the hardship. If they held a different set of expectations about large segments of their population they might be better equipped to make more ethical policies. Think about Guatemala or El Salvador. The distribution of income, land, jobs, and healthcare in those countries is so skewed in favor of the rich that the leadership must expect that the vast majority of the population is at least partially dissatisfied. It seems to me that to think otherwise is simply naive. So if you assume for a moment that the political leadership in those countries understands the problem, why then would they be so taken aback by the demands of the opposition? Wouldn't the entire situation be easier to defuse if the government simply held more reasoned expectations about the dissatisfaction and the potential demands of those who have much less? I think it would.

Fundamentally this is arguing that ill-conceived responses to opposition organizing and demonstrating could be avoided rather easily. The reliance on violent forms of repression seems to be unnecessary, not to mention shortsighted. But quite often that is the response of a government. Why do so many governments simply ignore, misinterpret, or fail to recognize where the critical political tensions lie in their countries? The easiest answer is politics. That is not completely satisfying. In many of the most repressive countries there is a small group that wields the vast majority of the political, military, and economic power, and they remain immune from the type of attention it would take to recognize the magnitude of the problems faced by the masses. If you focus on this long enough you'll begin to come to the conclusion that the greed of a few accounts for the suffering of many.

What would be an easier way out? Put yourself in the mindset of the political leadership in one of these countries. There is no doubt that democracy would matter, in part because the disenfranchised would be represented. At least you could reject the notion that a lack of knowledge accounted for the lack of foresight. But the Israelis missed the level of disaffection among the Palestinians during 2000. They seemed utterly surprised that the Palestinians would forgo a bad peace deal in return for four more years of violence. Miscalculation. If you were the enlightened leader of a poor country with a skewed distribution of resources, what would you do? The answer seems too easy. The cost of a civil war is just so much higher than the cost of heading off confrontation. The less costly approach is to institute reforms. This would be the rational way to deal with the problem, but it is not what many of these leaders do. It is almost as if their heads are buried in the sand. Greed, ignorance, callousness, righteousness—any of these explains their actions. But it is probably not what you or I would do, so why do they? Barbara Tuchman wrote a best-selling book called *The March of Folly* that might provide some of the answers. One of the primary explanations for the colossal blunders of political leaders, she said, was "wood-headedness." By wood-headedness she was referring to many things that get in the way of good choices, but two important ones are self-interest and an unwillingness to seriously consider the facts. If a government is not able to hold a realistic picture about the conditions of its people, then something like wood-headedness has to be operating. But there is more to it.

If we can get past the level of tolerance and lack of awareness, we come to the policies that provide the critical link for moving a pesky opposition into an armed rebellion. Political leaders can be intolerant, miss the important signals from the disgruntled population, and still make reasonable policy choices. How many of the demands would they have to agree to in order to defuse support for the cause? Probably not that many. Primarily they have to be smart enough not to try to put down the movement by force. The right choice is to negotiate their way out of the problem. Far too often political leaders try to fight their way out. Most indications suggest that this is a bad choice.

We don't all have to be our neighbor's keeper, nor for that matter do we have any obligation to work actively to prevent civil wars. In fact most of our understanding of what makes politics at the international level tick would suggest that worrying about such things is not important, maybe not even healthy. Let poverty be poverty, the abuses by governments their business. We have no obligation, no right, to do anything about these types of global problems. But there are other ways to approach this.

Many civil wars turn out to pose threats to global or regional stability, and so they end up being a problem even if you don't think your country has a role in preventing them. Most of what we know about politics in the global arena is that the breakdown of security is a bad thing. Just think of how the United States portrayed the potential for instability in Iraq in 2003. It was, according to President Bush, the instability in that country that might have led Saddam Hussein to develop and use nuclear weapons. It all turned out to be wrong, but the potential was enough, by his estimates, to warrant an intervention. If you run through the list of countries facing armed insurgencies you will find that their neighbors fear the risk that they face. From this vantage point it is the war itself that is the problem because it may spill over into another country, upset trading arrangements, or increase the risk of an international war. The strategic implications also play out through concerns over terrorism. It was no accident that Osama bin Laden and his Al Qaeda group could find safe haven in civil war–torn Afghanistan while they planned their assault on the World Trade Center and the Pentagon.

Even if there is no such thing as a moral imperative to change the conditions that lead to civil war, there remain good strategic and humanitarian reasons to stop them once they get started. The Israeli-Palestinian conflict is a great example of this. Just think of the human and material treasure that has gone into the last four years of the uprising. It is not only Israeli or Palestinian treasures that are at stake. Much of what we see as terrorism today appears to draw fire from the failure to act on the occupation of Palestine by the Israelis. Almost all Muslim extremist groups point to the policies of Israel as a prime motivation behind their actions. And many foreign leaders have made the case that ending the occupation is necessary to bring stability to the region and the globe. This is just one little civil war that really has not killed that many people. But it consumes an awful lot of energy around the world. Although some are skeptical, there are compelling reasons to link the tragedy of September 11, 2001, to the problem of Israeli occupation of the Palestinian Territories and the unwavering U.S. support for these policies.

Many political pundits will deny this link between the Israeli occupation and the events of September 11. We hear far too often from intelligent political leaders that Islamic fundamentalists just hate the freedoms that are represented by the United States. A book by a former CIA agent, *Imperial Hubris*, makes a compelling case that the policy community is simply missing all the obvious signals and cues. Most policy makers, in turn, deny that the author's views are correct. As the author says, the greatest mistake the policy community makes is to think that "radical Islamists attack us for what we think, not for what we do." The political leadership might be suffering from a bit of what Barbara Tuchman called "wood-headedness."

This little civil war in the middle of the Middle East is wreaking havoc around the world, and the world has sat back and watched for years as if there was nothing to be done. Far too much of the blame has been leveled at the late Palestinian leader Yasser Arafat. Some blame does lie with him and the Palestinians, but civil wars do not happen because only one side wants them. It takes a grievance and a bad set of policy choices to turn a poor situation into a disaster. It was Ariel Sharon who visited the Dome of the Rock in a provocative act that incited Palestinians in 2000. Palestinians were not happy with the way peace negotiations were going, but it also took a bad policy choice. Were there things that could have been done to stop this uprising long ago?

In many less visible ways this same basic problem plays out around the world. In the first two weeks of February 2005, Fuerzas Armadas Revolucionarias de Colombia (FARC) rebels in Colombia killed about sixty government troops. The United States has provided a multibillion-dollar military aid package to try to help the government stabilize the countryside. This civil war has been going on for nearly forty years, and another infusion of military aid will not convince the rebels to stop fighting. But clearly the United States is worried about the potential for a government defeat in Colombia. One of the problems is the drug trade from Colombia. Settling the civil war will potentially go a long way to making it hard on the drug traffickers. But Colombia is only one example. In the first few weeks of February 2005 about forty people were killed in the insurgency in the Philippines. To the United States this represents a vital part of the world, and again, this conflict has been going on for three decades. The United States sent troops, military advisors, and money, all of which will not bring a long-running insurgency to a halt. The countries that border the Democratic Republic of Congo have an interest in stability in that region, though you might be hard-pressed to see it by their policies. Far too often, it seems, those countries that get involved do so without concern for why the war started in the first place. These cases point us to the critical question of just what outsiders can do to bring these conflicts to an acceptable conclusion through negotiated settlement.

We have to remember that civil wars will end, whether or not members of the world community try to do something to stop them. It might take ten, twenty, or forty years, but eventually all wars stop. Key to thinking about whether and what to do is to consider the added costs of the war continuing for each additional year. Look at the civil war in Northern Ireland, the Troubles. After thirty years they managed to arrange a peace agreement with the help of U.S. mediation, and today the fighting has stopped. This war could probably have ended long ago if the two sides had been willing to make the necessary concessions, and some foreign leader willing to invest in the outcome. In rough terms about 135 people were killed and ten times as many wounded in each year of that conflict. It is never that linear, of course. No war ever is. But in total more than thirty-five hundred people were killed between 1968 and 1994. The war cost the British treasury over three billion pounds annually—at today's exchange rate this works out to well over five billion U.S. dollars per year. Each additional year without peace cost five billion dollars, one hundred thirty five souls, and one thousand three hundred and fifty injuries. The medical and social costs of the dead and the wounded are not included in these figures. Nor can you sum up the total costs by simply looking at the hospital or the treasury. Manufacturing employment in Northern Ireland declined by nearly 50 percent since the beginning of the conflict, about twice the decline of the rest of the United Kingdom.

I could give countless examples of conflicts around the world detailing the annual cost in human and material treasure. Each year that nothing is done to stop an ongoing civil war there are real costs that can be measured in terms of body counts, cash expenditures, or lost wages. How much are we willing to accept and how far are we willing to go? If there was nothing we could do these would be easy questions. When there is, they become more tragic.

The magnitude of the questions we face when thinking about civil wars sometimes perplexes me. The puzzlement comes not from whether we should or should not invest national or international resources in doing the right thing, but rather in the enormity of the problem at hand. Always trying to stop ongoing civil wars is a bit like fighting fires. It is not enough to be fighting fires the whole time. At some point you come to the conclusion that fire prevention will considerably reduce the workload on the fire department. There is little doubt in my mind that the firefighting role is possible, but the lack of political will and a continual drain on national resources will mean that none but the most pressing civil wars attract attention. Is there a better strategy? Intuition and evidence suggest that there is.

From my wandering of the globe and the times that I have stumbled into civil wars I have learned that the passion for justice—not equality, but justice—is fueled from deep down inside a group of people. Once some threshold is crossed, a threshold where people have decided to fight for change, military victory will at best delay the next uprising. The fight for justice will rear its head again. And the risks that people will take in pursuit of what they consider to be a more just outcome would boggle the mind of most of us in the wealthy and more stable parts of the world. You can beat that passion down, but you can never fully extinguish it. If it doesn't rise up in the current generation, it will in the next generation, or the one after. Violent suppression is but a short-term palliative. In short, if the world community does not address issues of poverty, poor health, the lack of education, government corruption, and the like, it will face a steady stream of brutal civil wars.

When it comes to thinking about obligations and potential actions, there is an important distinction between fighting for justice and fighting for equality. When people fight for justice they wish to prevent further exploitation. Fighting for equality implies that resources should be distributed equally. I spent time talking with members of the United Nicaraguan Opposition, the political wing of the Contra army, when they were fighting to overthrow the Sandinista government in Nicaragua. Never do I recall them making a demand for equality. Justice yes, equality no. The same was true of the people I spoke with in Guatemala, Nicaragua, and Honduras. They were not seeking equality. Kurds in Turkey seek justice, as do Palestinians in the Occupied Territories. There is an odd dimension to siding with those who are fighting against the call for justice. How do you justify defending injustice? Helping reach a negotiated settlement to a civil war might not result in the achievement of complete justice for the formerly aggrieved, but by virtue of negotiations the outcomes come closer to a just result than would a government achieving victory over rebels.

The pursuit of justice is not reserved for rebel armies; there are probably civil wars fought where the government has the call to justice on its side. But even if a government is on the right side of the question of justice, for the opposition to incur the risk of imprisonment, torture, and death they must think that they have a case worth fighting for. A negotiated outcome still seems like the most effective approach to settling the war.

There is always the worry that the cost of doing something proactive is too high given the political realities that leaders face. This, to me, is not the right way to think about trying to stop civil wars. When you get right down to it the costs are mostly political. Certainly any country that contributes to the material aspects of a peace agreement is going to have to dip into its treasury. There will be a cost. But all too often that same country will provide military support for one side in the war without due attention to trying to stop the conflict. That too has a cost. If the political will existed to entice rebel and government soldiers away from the battlefield, the right intervention strategies could be very effective. It would entail solving some of the underlying problems, but in the end it would be less costly than letting a conflict simmer for years. You don't have to think too far into the past to see the historical blunders that the world community has made in the Israeli-Palestinian conflict. It will end. And it will end with Israel relinquishing most or all of the pre-1967 territories to a Palestinian state. Israel will tear down settlements, move out settlers, and make some sort of arrangements over Jerusalem. It will have taken nearly thirty years of constant hostilities punctuated by extended periods of armed struggle, but it will get there.

We can always pose the question in hindsight as to whether they could have reached a settlement much earlier. Many would say yes. Many will blame the United States for its inability to constrain Israel. Some will blame Yasser Arafat, claiming that he preferred war to peace. And some will blame successive Israeli leaders for their belligerence, brutality, and settlement policies. But most will recognize that the conflict was prolonged by lack of political will to intervene effectively, inability to make concessions where necessary, and the unfortunate tendency to hold to a mistaken set of expectations about the opponent. Some other book will have to explore the reasons why all parties refused to budge. I struggle with the point that the United States could have done a better job of facilitating an agreement, if only there was the political will. The example is poignant because of the extreme costs of continued conflict, because of the intimate role of outside parties, and because of the strategic vulnerability of the region. But it is only one example. It is also an example of note because the fuel that fired the conflict turned on issues of justice, not equality. Is there a just settlement that will lead to an acceptable outcome, albeit an outcome that is not based on equality? The answer is most certainly yes, and it is the one that will eventually be obtained. But only after generations of conflict and a population filled with children of war. Darfur confronts us with a similar set of questions, as do the southern Philippines and, until recently, Northern Ireland and the Aceh in Indonesia.

A reasonable person may wonder how I got to this point. I certainly didn't start out here. I have elevated the need to act on structural poverty and civil war to the level of a moral obligation. My professional training does not provide much leeway to think about governments acting on the basis of moral commitments. The evidence does not provide the foundation for moral claims either. Only the individual can arrive at that point based on his or her individual values. Those periods of my life spent wandering streets and out-of-the-way haunts in countries caught up in the struggles and talking to the people on those troubled streets made the issues real. Looking at the evidence provided consistent patterns. Experience, intuition, and evidence have brought me to where I am. I promised the group in Guatemala who were fighting for justice and seeking information about their disappeared relatives that I would help them somehow. For twenty years I never knew how to. My experience there frightened me, their willingness to accept immense risk amazed me, and my own inability to match up to their standards disappointed me. I end up at this point because I think it is the right place to be.

Ending poverty or reducing the amount of political and economic discrimination is not going to end all civil wars for all time. These events are far too complex to hope for a simple solution. Removing economic motivations by providing more equitable access will, however, dramatically reduce the number of civil wars that we as a world community confront. Enough evidence that points in the same direction is hard to ignore. People rise up against their governments and are willing to take incredible risks in pursuit of change when the conditions under which they live are sufficiently marginal, and when expectations for the future are sufficiently bleak. Under these conditions the risks seem small. These are the situations that breed terrorists, insurgencies, and political chaos. These are also the conditions that make for weak markets, ensure high defense spending, and increasingly place a burden on international organizations such as the United Nations.

The road to civil wars is complex and long. There will be no divine inspiration that will show us how to stop them, but there are many exits along the way. The need to act is unquestionable, and coherent policies are possible. To allow civil wars to persist because political capital is lacking would be an unfortunate and, ultimately, self-destructive legacy.

If I have the same conversation with my son as I had with my father, today I would probably say the same words to him that my father said to me: There will be more wars in the years to come, and more famines to follow them. But perhaps, some day, there will be a different sort of conversation between another father and son in another time and place. That conversation may be different because we have begun to understand better the world we inhabit. Perhaps we understand that people pushed into that corner of despair and hopelessness will eventually shoot their way out of it, and from this we all stand to lose in some way. Perhaps, even though the pace of change is glacial, there is change, and the right policies will be born of the courage to apply knowledge to a contemporary dilemma.

POSTSCRIPT

Since completing my manuscript, one question has come up repeatedly: if structural poverty is at the core of my argument, I am asked, what can any one individual do to change the situation? This is a hard question to answer satisfactorily. Fundamentally the changes required to affect structural poverty are really big. And any one individual's contribution can only be small by comparison. I am also asked about the efficacy of the World Bank and the International Monetary Fund—two UN-based organizations designed to promote economic development.

Providing solutions for individuals to affect structural poverty might be more complex than the problem itself, and any solutions might also challenge the system that creates the problem in the first place. Because of these limitations, my effort will be tailored toward small contributions that individuals can make rather than ways for individuals to affect structural change.

First, I see the large-scale aid organizations doing more to perpetuate structural conditions than to alleviate them. Most organizations that grow to the size of the major donor outfits have, to a large extent, become part of the structure itself and therefore the changes they advocate miss the point. The International Monetary Fund and the World Bank are examples of this dilemma. They identify countries that have economic problems and those political and economic elites who seek large, very large, structural adjustment loans. In order for either of these organizations to get involved they demand political and/or economic changes that focus on creating "better" market conditions. In order to make these changes the borrowing countries quite often have to take subsidies and provisions away from the poorest just so that the wealthiest can borrow money.

Not a good way to change the structural conditions associated with poverty.

My solutions, therefore, involve smaller-scale initiatives that work more closely with the individual—both the individual recipient and the donor. Three alternative ways for individuals to get involved with the types of changes that will help alleviate some of the conditions that motivate people to rebel are (1) small, individually focused, antipoverty programs; (2) small-scale microfinance programs; and (3) support for those who advocate women's rights, worker's rights, and, more generally, human rights. None of these will fundamentally change the relationship between the structure that helps create the inequities and the people who suffer from them, but each can provide relief to individuals struggling at the margins. If these were really successful across a broad swath of countries, they might then begin to alter the structures that keep the poor impoverished.

There are a number of private not for profit organizations that help provide ways to allow individuals in developing countries to work their way out of poverty. To some degree these organizations introduce small-scale, relatively simple, technologies that people can use in the field. A key difference between these organizations and, say, the World Bank is that the World Bank advocates large and not easily serviceable technology that is much more useful for large-scale farming than for small-scale farming. These technologies tend to be targeted at the already well-off and in doing so exacerbates the structures that keep the poor poor. Small-scale farming requires inexpensive inputs, like irrigation pumps and milling processes, which can be purchased with little money and can be repaired in the field by local people. The efficiencies of scale are such that small farmers can make their lands productive and therefore resist the temptation to sell out to the large landowners. There are two such organizations with which I am familiar, and both have a track record of providing the means out of poverty in rural agricultural environments. They both work on the assumption that the local people, the poor in the countries in which they operate, want to work hard and if given access to the methods for doing so, they will work themselves out of poverty. The evidence suggests that these are very successful programs.

My wife and I have supported one such program called KickStart, headquartered in California and with offices in Kenya, Tanzania, and Mali. They have developed small scale technologies and have successfully trained local farmers and merchants to adapt them to local environments. Another organization with a very similar pedigree is International Development Enterprises (IDE), with offices in Colorado and regional offices in eight countries. The former director of IDE, Paul Polak, has recently written a book about poverty in which he describes some simple but effective ways to think about and address the problems. Both of these outfits provide a way for individual donors to connect with individual solutions.

KickStart International
2435 Polk Street, Suite 20
San Francisco, CA 94109-1600

International Development Enterprises
10403 West Colfax, Suite 500
Lakewood, CO 80215

Microfinance organizations also provide a way for individual donors to get money directly into the hands of individuals who need access to small amounts of start up capital. Microfinance involves very small loans to people in developing countries. Sometimes these loans are administered through formal banks, but the internet provides ways for individuals to loan directly to individuals in need. The payback rate on microfinance loans is very high by almost any standard, and most evidence will point to a very high success rate in terms of the people using the money they borrow to develop projects that can provide continuing income. Microfinance originally started out as loans to women who needed the money to purchase the materials for a weaving business, milling tools for a bakery, and such small-scale businesses. Microfinance has advanced beyond this initial emphasis and today there are quite extensive networks. Since these are organized as loans rather than grants, it is more like small scale investments, quite often avoiding banks that charge excessive interest or loan sharks who exploit rather than help the people to whom they loan money. One Internet microlender is Kiva (http://www.kiva.org), which actually puts the donor directly in touch with the borrower, and the amounts can be as low as twenty-five dollars. They give information on the payback rate of various borrowers and let you set the amount you want to lend. Other, more well-known and considerably larger-scale operations include the Grameen Bank of Bangladesh (http://www.grameen-info.org), whose founder won the 2006 Nobel Peace Prize, and FINCA (http://www.villagebanking.org), a U.S.-based microfinance organization.

One of the more structural aspects of poverty can be found in the inability of people to organize to demand living wages, or in many instances, the rights of women to get an education or work. Sweatshops, child labor, and worker intimidation are regular stories in the mainstream media. The campaign against Nike involving child labor, the textile and clothing industry because of sweatshop conditions, the campaign to get Coke to stop intimidating workers at its plants around the world, are all examples of how human rights influence the conditions of poverty. You don't have to be prounion to understand the consequences of child labor, sweatshops, or executions of labor organizers. When children are compelled to work to survive at the expense of going to school, they are destined to a life not much better than the conditions under which they started working.

A number of organizations work for the right to organize, to ban child labor and sex slavery, for the opportunity for girls to get an education. Helping these types of groups can, in small ways, help create the conditions for people to get out of poverty. Two names—The Campaign for Labor Rights (http://www.clrlabor.org/index.htm) and Urgent Action Fund (http://www.urgentactionfund.org), which helps to promote the rights of women around the world. Of course there is Amnesty International, the well-regarded organization that uses public campaigns to challenge governments that torture or abuse their citizens (http://www.amnesty.org). Their general approach is to get people worldwide to write letters on behalf of prisoners of conscience as a way of pressuring governments into releasing them.

However any one individual chooses to act in pursuit of changing the living conditions for people around the globe, the key thing is that some action is generally better than not making any effort at all. But you also have to be realistic in terms of what you can expect these small steps to do. Although they may not directly change the structure of the systems that generate the poverty so prevalent around the world, over time a lot of small steps and individual efforts can translate into change that is perceptible.

SOCIAL INDICATORS OF ECONOMIC DEVELOPMENT FOR COUNTRIES DISCUSSED IN THIS BOOK

Country	Human Development Rank	Life Expectancy at Birth	Adult Literacy (% over age 15)
Algeria	108	69.5	68.9
Angola	166	40.1	42.0
Burma	132	57.2	85.3
Burundi	173	40.8	50.4
Central African Republic	169	39.8	48.6
Chad	167	44.7	45.8
Colombia	73	72.1	92.1
Côte d'Ivoire	Not reporting	Not reporting	Not reporting
Democratic Republic of the Congo	168	41.4	62.7
Ethiopia	170	45.5	41.5
India	127	63.7	61.3
Indonesia	111	66.6	87.9
Israel[1]	22/102	79.1/72.3	95.3/90.2
Liberia	Not reporting	Not reporting	Not reporting
Nepal	140	59.6	44.0
Philippines	83	69.8	92.6
Russia	57	66.7	99.6
Rwanda	159	38.9	69.2
Somalia	Not reporting	Not reporting	Not reporting
Sudan	139	55.5	59.9
Turkey	88	70.4	86.5
Uganda	146	45.7	68.9
United States	8	77.0	99.0
France	16	78.9	99.0

The data for the United States and France are shown for comparison purposes.

1. Israel/Occupied Territories

Country	School Enrollment Rate	Infant Mortality Rate (% of live births)	Percent below the Poverty Line of $2/Day
Algeria	70	3.9	15.1
Angola	30	15.4	Not reporting
Burma	48	7.7	Not reporting
Burundi	33	11.4	89.2
Central African Republic	31	11.5	84.0
Chad	35	11.7	Not reporting
Colombia	68	1.9	22.6
Côte d'Ivoire	Not Reporting	Not reporting	Not reporting
Democratic Republic of the Congo	27	12.9	Not reporting
Ethiopia	34	11.4	80.7
India	61.3	6.7	79.9
Indonesia	65	3.3	52.4
Israel[1]	92/79	0.6/2.3	Not reporting
Liberia	Not Reporting	Not reporting	Not reporting
Nepal	61	6.6	82.5
Philippines	81	2.9	46.4
Russia	88	1.8	Not reporting
Rwanda	53	9.6	84.6
Somalia	Not Reporting	Not reporting	Not reporting
Sudan	36	1.8	Not reporting
Turkey	68	3.6	10.3
Uganda	71	8.2	Not reporting
United States	92	0.7	Not reporting
France	91	0.4	Not reporting

The data for the United States and France are shown for comparison purposes.

1. Israel/Occupied Territories

Source: Data from the UN Development Program, *Human Development Report, 2004* (New York: UNDP 2004).

FURTHER READING

Poverty, Grievances, and Civil War

Collier, Paul. *The Bottom Billion: Why the Poorest Countries Are Failing and What Can Be Done about It.* Oxford: Oxford University Press, 2007.

Collier, Paul, V. L. Elliot, Havard Hegre, Anke Hoeffler, Marta Reynal-Querol, and Nicholas Sambanis. *Breaking the Conflict Trap: Civil War and Development Policy.* Washington, DC: World Bank, 2003.

Collier, Paul, and Anke Hoeffler. "On the Incidence of Civil War in Africa." *Journal of Conflict Resolution* 46, no. 1 (2002): 13–28.

Elbadawi, Ibrahim A., and Nicholas Sambanis. "Why Are There So Many Civil Wars in Africa? Understanding and Preventing Violent Conflict." *Journal of African Economies* 9, no. 3 (2000): 244–269.

Fearon, James D. "Commitment Problems and the Spread of Ethnic Conflict." In *The International Spread of Ethnic Conflict: Fear, Diffusion, and Escalation,* ed. David A. Lake and Donald S. Rothchild. Princeton, NJ: Princeton University Press, 1998.

Fearon, James D., and D. D. Laitin. "Ethnicity, Insurgency, and Civil War." *American Political Science Review* 97, no. 1 (2003): 75–90.

Gurr, Ted Robert. *Why Men Rebel.* New Haven, CT: Yale University Press, 1970.

Gurr, Ted Robert, and Will H. Moore. "Ethnopolitical Rebellion: A Cross-Sectional Analysis of the 1980s with Risk Assessment of the 1990s." *American Journal of Political Science* 41, no. 4 (1997): 1079–1103.

Heath, Julie, David Mason, William Smith, and Joseph Weingarten. "The Calculus of Fear: Revolution, Repression, and the Rational Peasant." *Social Science Quarterly* 81, no. 2 (2000): 622–633.

Hegre, Havard, Tania Ellingsen, Scott Gates, and Nils Petter Gleditsch. "Toward a Democratic Civil Peace? Democracy, Political Change, and Civil War, 1816–1992." *American Political Science Review* 95, no. 1 (2001): 33–48.

Horowitz, Donald L. *Ethnic Groups in Conflict.* Berkeley: University of California Press, 1985.

Huntington, Samuel. *Political Order in Changing Societies.* New Haven, CT: Yale University Press, 1968.

David Lake. "International Relations Theory and Internal Conflict." *International Studies Review* 5, no. 4 (2003): 81–90.

Lake, David A., and Donald Rothchild. "Spreading Fear: The Genesis of Transnational Ethnic Conflict." In *The International Spread of Ethnic Conflict: Fear, Diffusion, and Escalation,* ed. David A. Lake and Donald S. Rothchild. Princeton, NJ: Princeton University Press, 1998.

Mason, T. David. *Caught in the Crossfire.* Lanham, MD: Rowman and Littlefield, 2004.

Midlarsky, Manus I. "Rulers and the Ruled: Patterned Inequality and the Onset of Mass Political Violence." *American Political Science Review* 82, no. 2 (June 1988): 491–509.

Muller, Edward N., Mitchell A. Seligson, Hung-der Fu, and Manus I. Midlarsky. "Land Inequality and Political Violence." *American Political Science Review* 83, no. 2 (June 1989): 577–596.

Polak, Paul. *Out of Poverty: What Works When Traditional Approaches Fail.* San Francisco: Berrett-Koehler, 2008.

Regan, Patrick M., and Daniel Norton. "Greed, Grievance, and Mobilization in Civil Wars." *Journal of Conflict Resolution* 49, no. 3 (2005): 319–336.

Mobilization of Rebels and Resources

Azam, Jean-Paul. "The Redistributive State and Conflicts in Africa." *Journal of Peace Research* 38, no. 4 (2001): 429–444.

Bussmann, Margit, and Gerald Schneider. "When Globalization Discontent Turns Violent: Foreign Economic Liberalization and Internal War." *International Studies Quarterly* 51 (2007): 79–97.

Collier, Paul. "Rebellion as a Quasi-Criminal Activity." *Journal of Conflict Resolution* 44, no. 6 (2000): 839–853.

DeNardo, James. *Power in Numbers: Political Strategy of Protest and Rebellion.* Princeton, NJ: Princeton University Press, 1985.

Gates, Scott. "Recruitment and Allegiance: The Microfoundations of Rebellion." *Journal of Conflict Resolution* 46, no. 1 (2002): 111–130.

Grossman, Herschel I. "A General Equilibrium Model of Insurrections." *American Economic Review* 81, no. 4 (1991): 912–921.

Lichbach, Mark Irving. *The Rebel's Dilemma.* Ann Arbor: University of Michigan Press, 1995.

———. "What Makes Rational Peasants Revolutionary: Dilemma, Paradox, and Irony in Peasant Collective Action." *World Politics* 46, no. 3 (1994): 383–418.

———. "Will Rational People Rebel against Inequality? Samson's Choice." *American Journal of Political Science* 34, no. 4 (1990): 1049–1076.

Olson, Mancur. *The Logic of Collective Action: Public Goods and the Theory of Groups.* Cambridge, MA: Harvard University Press, 1971.

Popkin, Samuel. *The Rational Peasant: The Political Economy of Rural Society.* Berkeley: University of California Press, 1979.

Tarrow, Sidney. 1994. *Power in Movements: Social Movements and Contentious Politics.* New York: Cambridge University Press, 1994.

Tilly, Charles. *From Mobilization to Revolution.* Reading, MA: Addison-Wesley, 1978.

Weinstein, Jeremy M. *Inside Rebellion: The Politics of Insurgent Violence.* Cambridge, UK: Cambridge University Press, 2007.

Social Groups, Ethnicity, and Culture

Carment, David. "The Ethnic Dimensions in World Politics." *Third World Quarterly* 15, no. 4 (1994): 551–582.

Davis, David R., and Will H. Moore. "Ethnicity Matters: Transnational Ethnic Alliances and Foreign Policy Behavior." *International Studies Quarterly* 41, no. 1 (1997): 171–184.

Elbadawi, Ibrahim A., and Nicholas Sambanis. "Why Are There So Many Civil Wars in Africa? Understanding and Preventing Violent Conflict." *Journal of African Economies* 9, no. 3 (2000): 244–269.

Ellingsen, Tanja. "Colorful Community or Ethnic Witches' Brew? Multiethnicity and Domestic Conflict during and after the Cold War." *Journal of Conflict Resolution* 44, no. 2 (2000): 228–249.

Fearon, James D. "Commitment Problems and the Spread of Ethnic Conflict." In *The International Spread of Ethnic Conflict: Fear, Diffusion, and*

Escalation, ed. David A. Lake and Donald S. Rothchild. Princeton, NJ: Princeton University Press, 1998.

Fearon, James D., and D. D. Laitin. "Ethnicity, Insurgency, and Civil War." *American Political Science Review* 97, no. 1 (2003): 75–90.

Forbes, H. D. *Ethnic Conflict: Commerce, Culture, and the Contact Hypothesis.* New Haven, CT: Yale University Press, 1997.

Fox, Jonathon. *Religion, Civilization, and Civil War.* Lanham, MD: Lexington Books, 2004.

Gurr, Ted Robert. *Minorities at Risk: A Global View of Ethnopolitical Conflicts.* Washington, DC: United States Institute of Peace, 1993.

———. *People versus States: Minorities at Risk in the New Century.* Washington, DC: United States Institute of Peace, 2000.

Gurr, Ted Robert, and Barbara Harff. *Ethnic Conflict in World Politics.* Boulder, CO: Westview Press, 2000.

Horowitz, Donald L. *Ethnic Groups in Conflict.* Berkeley: University of California Press, 1985.

Kaufmann, Chaim. "Possible and Impossible Solutions to Ethnic Conflicts." *International Security* 20, no. 4 (1996): 136–175.

Reynal-Querol, Marta. "Ethnicity, Political Systems, and Civil Wars." *Journal of Conflict Resolution* 46, no. 1 (2002): 29–54.

Sambanis, Nicholas. "Do Ethnic and Non-Ethnic Wars Have the Same Causes?" *Journal of Conflict Resolution* 45, no. 3 (2001): 259–282.

Szayna, Thomas S., and Ashley J. Tellis. Introduction to *Identifying Potential Ethnic Conflict: Application of a Process Model,* ed. Thomas S. Szayna. Santa Monica, CA: Rand, 2000.

Government Responses to Political Opposition

Gartner, Scott S., and Patrick M. Regan. "Threat and Repression: The Non-Linear Relationship between Government and Opposition Violence." *Journal of Peace Research* 33, no. 3 (August 1996): 273–287.

Gurr, Ted Robert. *Why Men Rebel.* New Haven, CT: Yale University Press, 1970.

Hegre, Havard, Tania Ellingsen, Scott Gates, and Nils Petter Gleditsch. "Toward a Democratic Civil Peace? Democracy, Political Change, and Civil War, 1816–1992." *American Political Science Review* 95, no. 1 (2001): 33–48.

Henderson, Errol A., and J. David Singer. "Civil War in the Post-Colonial World, 1946–92." *Journal of Peace Research* 37, no. 3 (2000): 275–299.

Krain, Matthew, and Marissa Edson Myers. "Democracy and Civil War: A Note on the Democratic Peace Proposition." *International Interactions* 23, no. 1 (1997): 109–118.

Mason, T. David, and Dale Krane. "The Political Economy of Death Squads." *International Studies Quarterly* 33, no. 2 (1989): 175–198.

Moore, Will H. "Repression and Dissent: Substitution, Context, and Timing." *American Journal of Political Science* 42, no. 3 (1998): 851–873.

———. "The Repression of Dissent: A Substitution Model of Government Coercion." *Journal of Conflict Resolution* 44, no. 1 (2000): 107–127.

Regan, Patrick M., and Errol A. Henderson. "Democracy, Threats, and Political Repression in Developing Countries: Are Democracies Internally Less Violent?" *Third World Quarterly* 23, no. 1 (2002): 119–136.

Regan, Patrick M., and Daniel Norton. "Greed, Grievance, and Mobilization in Civil Wars." *Journal of Conflict Resolution* 49, no. 3 (2005): 319–336.

Sisk, Timothy D. *Power Sharing and International Mediation in Ethnic Conflicts.* Washington, DC: United States Institute of Peace, 1996.

Wantchekon, Leonard. "The Paradox of 'Warlord' Democracy: A Theoretical Investigation." *American Political Science Review* 9, no. 1 (2004): 17–33.

Wantchekon, Leonard, and Zvika Neeman. "A Theory of Post–Civil War Democratization." *Journal of Theoretical Politics* 14 (2002): 439–464.

Wood, Jean Elisabeth. "An Insurgent Path to Democracy: Popular Mobilization, Economic Interests, and Regime Transition in South Africa and El Salvador." *Comparative Political Studies* 34, no. 8 (2001): 862–888.

Yalcin Mousseau, Demet. "Democratizing with Ethnic Divisions: A Source of Conflict?" *Journal of Peace Research* 38, no. 5 (2001): 547–567.

The Consequences of Civil War

Barnett, Michael. *Eyewitness to a Genocide.* Ithaca, NY: Cornell University Press, 2002.

Berkeley, Bill. *The Graves Are Not Yet Full: Race, Tribe, and Power in the Heart of Africa.* New York: Basic Books, 2001.

Collier, Paul, V. L. Elliot, Havard Hegre, Anke Hoeffler, Marta Reynal-Querol, and Nicholas Sambanis. *Breaking the Conflict Trap: Civil War and Development Policy.* Washington, DC: World Bank, 2003.

Davenport, Christian A., Will H. Moore, and Steven C. Poe. "Sometimes You Just Have to Leave: Threat and Refugee Movements, 1964–1989." *International Interactions* 29, no. 1 (2003): 27–55.

Gourrevitch, Philip. *We Wish to Inform You That Tomorrow We Will Be Killed with Our Families*. London: Picador, 1998.

Murdoch, James C., and Todd Sandler. "Economic Growth, Civil Wars, and Spatial Spillovers." *Journal of Conflict Resolution* 46, no. 1 (2002): 91–110.

Pape, Robert. *Dying to Win*. New York: Random House, 2005.

Rummell, Rudolph. "Democracy, Power, Genocide, and Mass Murder." *Journal of Conflict Resolution* 39, no. 1 (1995): 3–26.

Interventions, Peacekeeping Operations, and the End of Civil Wars

Carment, David, and Dane Rowlands. "Three's Company." *Journal of Conflict Resolution* 42, no. 5 (1998): 572–599.

Elbadawi, Ibrahim A. "Civil Wars and Poverty: The Role of External Interventions, Political Rights, and Economic Growth." Paper presented at the World Bank conference "Civil Conflicts, Crime, and Violence," Washington, DC, February 22–23, 1999.

Enterline, Andrew, and Dylan Balch-Lyndsay. "Killing Time: The World Politics of Civil War Duration." *International Studies Quarterly* 44, no. 4 (2000): 615–642.

Fortna, Virginia Page. "Does Peacekeeping Keep Peace? International Intervention and the Duration of Peace after Civil War." *International Studies Quarterly* 48, no. 2 (2004): 269–292.

Gent, Stephen. "Strange Bedfellows: Major Power Intervention in Civil Conflicts." *Journal of Politics* 69, no. 4 (2007): 1089–1102.

Hampson, Fen Osler. *Nurturing Peace: Why Peace Settlements Succeed or Fail*. Washington, DC: United States Institute of Peace, 1996.

Hartzell, Caroline. "Explaining the Stability of Negotiated Settlements to Intrastate Wars." *Journal of Conflict Resolution* 43, no. 1 (1999): 3–22.

Hartzell, Caroline, Matthew Hoddie, and Donald Rothchild. "Stabilizing the Peace after Civil War: An Investigation of Some Key Variables." *International Organization* 55, no. 1 (2001): 183–208.

Kaufmann, Chaim. "Possible and Impossible Solutions to Ethnic Conflicts." *International Security* 20, no. 4 (1996): 136–175.

Kydd, Andrew. "Which Side Are You On? Bias, Credibility, and Mediation." *American Journal of Political Science* 47, no. 4 (2003): 597–611.

Pillar, Paul R. *Negotiating Peace: War Termination as a Bargaining Process.* Princeton, NJ: Princeton University Press, 1983.

Powell, Robert. *In the Shadow of Power.* Princeton, NJ: Princeton University Press, 1999.

Regan, Patrick M. "Choosing to Intervene: Outside Interventions into Internal Conflicts as a Policy Choice." *Journal of Politics* 60, no. 3 (1998): 754–779.

———. *Civil Wars and Foreign Powers.* Ann Arbor: University of Michigan Press, 2002.

———. "Conditions of Successful Third Party Intervention in Intra-State Conflicts." *Journal of Conflict Resolution* 40, no. 1 (1996): 336–359.

———. "Third Party Interventions and the Duration of Intrastate Conflict." *Journal of Conflict Resolution* 46, no. 1 (2002): 55–73.

Regan, Patrick, and Aysegul Aydin. "Diplomacy and Other Forms of Intervention." *Journal of Conflict Resolution* 50, no. 5 (2006): 736–756.

Rosenau, James N. "The Concept of Intervention." *Journal of International Affairs* 22 (1968): 165–176.

———. "Intervention as a Scientific Concept." *Journal of Conflict Resolution* 13, no. 2 (1969): 149–171.

Sambanis, Nicholas. "Partition as a Solution to Ethnic War: An Empirical Critique of the Theoretical Literature." *World Politics* 52, no. 4 (2000): 437–483.

Wagner, Robert Harrison. "The Causes of Peace." In *Stopping the Killing: How Civil Wars End,* ed. Roy Licklider. New York: New York University Press, 1993.

Walter, Barbara. *Committing to Peace.* Princeton, NJ: Princeton University Press, 2002.

Wood, Elizabeth. *Forging Democracy from Below.* New York: Cambridge University Press, 2000.

Woodward, Susan. "Economic Priorities for Successful Peace Implementation." In *Ending Civil Wars,* ed. Stephen John Stedman, Donald Rothchild, and Elizabeth M. Cousens. Boulder, CO: Lynne Rienner, 2002.

Zartman, I. William. "Dynamics and Constraints in Negotiations in Internal Conflicts." In *Elusive Peace: Negotiating an End to Civil Wars,* ed. I. William Zartman. Washington, DC: Brookings Institution, 1995.

INDEX

Peace and Freedom Party, 102
Peace Corps, 84
Peacekeepers, 165, 166, 168, 169, 170, 172
Peacekeeping, 162, 169, 172, 177–178
Peacemaking, 164, 168
Peace process, 139, 161, 177
Peace Research Institute, 32
Per capita income, 33–34, 35, 38, 69, 120
Perón, Eva, 29
Perón, Juan, 29
Philippines, 34, 156, 183, 200; deaths in, 2, 196; rich-to-poor ratios in, 48
"Physical integrity of person" indicators, 113
Plaza de Mayo, 29
Polak, Paul, 205
Police, 171, 175, 177
Polio, eliminating, 190
Political access, 176, 182
Political arrangements, 128, 153, 176
Political challenges, responding to, 116–117
Political changes, 102, 103, 108, 128, 172
Political influence, 9, 120
Political issues, 74, 129
Political movements, 8, 100, 134
Political prisoners, 115, 192
Political process, 106, 175, 176, 177–178, 180; building, 177; civil wars and, 110; negotiations and, 103
Political will, 129, 182, 198, 200
Politics, 80, 193; cultural identity and, 97; economic issues and, 56, 96; global, 195; international, 134; poverty and, 9, 18, 96, 98; resource distribution and, 99; revolution and, 75; self-interest and, 184
Poor: motivations for, 39; political process and, 18; struggles of, 61; subsidies for, 98
Poor countries: corruption and, 186;

extreme wealth in, 41–42; infrastructure of, 117
Poverty, 58, 68, 88, 130, 178, 193, 198, 204; absolute, 42, 43, 46, 50; addressing, 21, 190; amidst wealth, 38, 40, 41, 42, 47; causes of, 7, 28; civil wars and, 9, 16–17, 21, 23, 24, 29, 31, 33, 38, 39 (fig.), 52, 70, 71, 116, 129, 186, 187, 188; conditions of, 72; contributions to, 190; cultural, 9; data about, 35, 71; dilemma of, 7, 11, 31, 38, 185; economic, 24, 28, 39, 40, 201; enduring, 25, 61, 120, 138, 188; extreme, 121; global, 25, 188, 189; impact of, 65, 121; intention and, 16; learning about, 27; local, 188; national, 188; politics and, 9, 18, 96, 98; real, 20, 188; reducing, 3, 6, 185, 186, 187, 189, 190, 191, 201; relative, 46; resource pool and, 62; situational, 21, 27, 28; social, 9, 19, 24; structural, 18, 21, 23, 24, 27, 28, 52, 83, 187, 188, 189, 200, 203, 204, 206
Poverty line, 34; percent below for various countries, 211 (table)
Power, 16, 83; abuse of, 178; distribution of, 103, 114–115, 141; economic clout and, 80; gaining, 97; political, 175; relationships, 10; relinquishing, 120, 160; resources and, 98, 99, 100
Protestants, Catholics and, 44, 71, 82, 93, 95, 96, 99
Protests, 51, 68, 109; motivations for, 116; violent crimes and, 102

Quilali, 15, 24, 34, 91, 92, 135, 147

Ramallah, 6, 45, 133
Rape, 129, 168, 178, 180, 185; as political tool, 123–124; systematic, 88, 124, 125
Reagan, Ronald, 57, 63, 136, 140
Rebel armies, 24, 82, 83; confronting, 46, 188; disarmament of, 162, 166, 173; joining, 23–24, 55, 73–74, 91,

Smallpox, eliminating, 190
SNCC. *See* Student Non-Violent Coordinating Committee
Social conditions, 8, 9, 32, 45, 50, 128
Social security, 27, 34
Social welfare, 71
Somalia, 71; civil war in, 123, 148; intervention in, 134, 136; UN forces in, 164–165
South Africa: apartheid in, 22, 99; Blacks in, 47; unequal conditions in, 43; wealth distribution in, 49
Sri Lanka, 2, 6, 21, 124, 159, 183, 191; suicide bombers in, 5
Stability, 112; civil wars and, 194–195; global/regional, 148, 194–195, 197
Stable points, 160
Stagnation, 68, 69
Steinbeck, John, 51, 90
Structural adjustments, 25, 175, 203
Structural conditions, 18, 24, 128, 190
Student Non-Violent Coordinating Committee (SNCC), 102
Students for a Democratic Society (SDS), 102
Sudan, 31, 34, 72, 159, 161, 183, 191; Arabs in, 96; Blacks in, 47, 96; casualties in, 2, 162; civil war in, 122, 148, 173; conflict in, 82; indicators in, 70; negotiations in, 162
Suicide bombers, 5, 8, 168
Sunnis, struggle of, 45
Sweatshops, 206

Taliban, 134, 142
Tamil, 21, 93
Tax rates, 97
Tax relief, 98
Taylor, Charles: civil war and, 87–88
Technology, 139, 204
Terror, 107, 109, 114, 201; reducing, 99, 104
Tikal region, 86
Torture, 107, 112, 115, 116, 122, 179, 192, 199

Tourism, 11, 54, 143
Tribunals, 179, 180
Troubles, 82, 103, 197
Trust, 168, 172
Truth and Reconciliation Commission, 180
Truth commissions, 178, 179, 180, 182
Tuchman, Barbara, 194, 196
Tul Karm, 45
Turkey: inflation in, 65; Kurds in, 47, 84, 199
Turks, 47; Kurds and, 84
Tutsis, 143; Hutus and, 79–80, 165

Uganda, deaths in, 2
UNDP. *See* United Nations Development Program
UN Development Program (UNDP), 32, 120, 121; data from, 56, 127; report by, 35, 70–71
UNHCR. *See* United Nations High Commission for Refugees
UN High Commission for Refugees (UNHCR), 125, 126
Union army, 178
Unions, 63, 105, 108, 157
United Nations, 1, 32, 48, 80, 169, 173–174, 201; Cambodia and, 174; civil wars and, 31, 165, 166; data from, 46; intervention by, 163–164; Nicaragua and, 174; peace process and, 177, 181; per capita income levels and, 38; resolutions by, 133; Somalia and, 164–165
United Nicaraguan Opposition, 199
United States: Blacks in, 47; occupation by, 112–113; unequal conditions in, 43
UN Security Council, Rwanda and, 79
Uppsala University, data from, 32, 46, 48, 56
Urgent Action Fund, 206
Urquhart, Sir Brian, 163, 165, 182
U.S. Agency for International Development (USAID), 114

ABOUT THE AUTHOR

Patrick M. Regan is Professor of Political Science at Binghamton University. He studies the ways in which civil wars can be stopped. He has written two other books and numerous articles on managing conflicts, started two novels that remain unfinished, and traveled extensively around the world.

 Mark A. Boyer, University of Connecticut, Series Editor

Titles in the Series

Forthcoming